AMELIA LOST

The LIFE and DISAPPEARANCE of AMELIA EARHART

by CANDACE FLEMING

LETTERING by JESSICA HISCHE

A YEARLING BOOK

Visit us on the Web! rhcbooks.com
Educators and librarians, for a variety of teaching tools, visit us at RHTeachersLibrarians.com

Library of Congress Cataloging-in-Publication Data is available upon request.
ISBN 978-0-375-84198-9 (hc)
ISBN 978-0-375-94598-4 (glb)
ISBN 978-0-307-98021-2 (ebook)
ISBN 978-0-593-17784-6 (pb)

A NOTE ON THE TYPE: The text of this book was set in a typeface called Electra, which was designed in 1935
by William Addison Dwiggins. The subchapter headings, sidebar titles, and first lines were set in Mostra Nuova,
designed by Mark Simonson and inspired by 1930s Italian Art Deco poster lettering.

Printed in the United States of America
10 9 8 7 6 5
First Yearling Edition 2019

ACKNOWLEDGMENTS

No project can take wing without the help of a talented flight crew. My copilots on this adventure were:

Ric Gillespie, executive director of The International Group for Historic Aircraft Recovery (TIGHAR), who patiently answered my endless questions; generously allowed me unlimited access to his organization's remarkable collection of primary documents, scientific articles and historic photographs; and meticulously fact-checked the completed manuscript. I could never have uncovered the truth about the search for Amelia Earhart or reconstructed the day-to-day events without his boundless knowledge and expertise.

James O'Donnell at the Smithsonian National Postal Museum, who burrowed through the archives to uncover a rare 1937 signed Amelia Earhart stamp cover.

Alan Sponheimer and the Ames Historical Society, whose admiration for Neta Snook and her place in aviation history translated to the pages of this book.

Diana Carey, reference librarian at the Schlesinger Library, who time and again found exactly what I was looking for.

Carl Snow, librarian, who guided me through the vast holdings of Purdue University's Special Collections, answering questions and hunting down photos.

Scott Fleming for his technical savvy.

And last but not least, my amazing editor, Ann Kelley, and my equally amazing book designer, Rachael Cole. I'm blessed to have flown with you!

CONTENTS

Sometimes it's hard to tell fact from fiction. Time and again, I unearthed a telling incident or charming anecdote only to learn that it wasn't true. Frustrating? You bet. But it was also enlightening, a reminder that it is often difficult to find the history in the hype, to separate truth from myth.

And as I learned, much of Amelia Earhart's story is myth. Take, for instance, the often-repeated story of the flier's first glimpse of an airplane. According to Earhart, this happened at the Iowa State Fair in 1908 when she was just eleven years old. "It was a thing of wire and wood," she wrote in her memoir, *The Fun of It.* "I was much more interested in an absurd hat made of an inverted peach basket which I purchased for fifteen cents."

It's a charming story.

But placed in the context of aviation history, it can't possibly be true. Just five years earlier, in December 1903, Wilbur and Orville Wright had made their first bumbling flight. For the next four years, the brothers had busied themselves refining their flying machine and applying for patents. Not until 1908 did they begin flying in public again, and neither of them flew anywhere near Iowa. Wilbur made demonstration flights in France, while Orville flew in Virginia for the U.S. Army Signal Corps. The only other flying being done at this time was by a Frenchman named Henri Farman, but his were only very short flights in a very straight line.

Why would Amelia make up such a story?

Because she was a celebrity with an image to maintain, and almost everything she told the public was meant to enhance that image. "I must continue to be a heroine in the public eye," she once said, "otherwise flying opportunities will stop rolling in." So Amelia Earhart (along with her husband, George Putnam) took an active role in mythologizing her own life. She led the public to believe that her famous tousled hair was naturally curly, when in fact she took a curling iron to it each day. She impressed the media with her quiet and demure attitude, when in truth she was forthright and outspoken. And yes, she occasionally told fibs. In short, she left behind layer upon layer of myth and legend.

For two years I chipped away at those layers. And the person I eventually uncovered surprised me. Amelia Earhart was so much more than a pilot. She was a savvy businesswoman (and cutthroat competitor when necessary); a popular lecturer; a fashion icon; the author of three books and countless magazine articles; a contributing editor at *Cosmopolitan* magazine and a correspondent for the *New York Herald-Tribune*; and a women's career consultant at Purdue University. But most important, she symbolized the new opportunities awaiting women in the twentieth century. Remarked Eleanor Roosevelt, "She helped the cause of women by giving them a feeling that there was nothing they could not do."

The MORNING HOURS

ON THE MORNING OF JULY 2, 1937, the coast guard cutter *Itasca* drifted on the Pacific Ocean, waiting . . . listening. . . .

Hundreds of miles to the west, the famous female pilot Amelia Earhart was winging her way toward Howland Island—a narrow spit of coral sand just to the west of the ship. On this tiny dot of land, a handful of laborers had hastily built a runway just for Earhart, because she needed a place to land and refuel during the last leg of her around-the-world flight.

The coast guard cutter Itasca *standing by at Howland Island.*

Amelia Earhart's plane wings its way over Asia, June 1937.

But finding Howland Island from the air was a difficult task. Only two miles long and a half mile wide, Howland sits in the middle of the vast Pacific Ocean. "Only the most highly skilled and experienced fliers could ever have spotted it," remarked one sailor aboard *Itasca*.

This was the reason the cutter was standing by. The crew hoped to help Earhart by making the island easier to spot. At midnight, searchlights had been switched on, serving as a beacon for the plane in case it picked up a tailwind and arrived early. At dawn, the ship's boilers had taken over, belching out thick black clouds of smoke as a visual signal.

Where's Howland?

To see how difficult it is to spot Howland Island from the air, watch the Waitt Institute for Discovery's video at http://log.searchforamelia.org/wow-wheres-howland.

Leo Bellarts tried to contact Amelia Earhart's plane from this radio room aboard Itasca.

Meanwhile, the ship's radio stood ready to send and receive messages. Chief Radioman Leo Bellarts himself had checked to make sure the transmitters and receivers were working properly. Earlier it had been agreed that Earhart would send her radio call letters—KHAQQ—and any other necessary flight information on 3105 kilocycles (similar to a radio channel). In this way, plane and ship hoped to stay in contact. But *Itasca* didn't hear from Earhart until 2:45 a.m. "Cloudy and overcast," she calmly reported. The rest of her message was lost in static.

For the past several hours *Itasca* had been sending Earhart the Morse code letter "A"—another aid to help guide her to the island. But if she heard this signal, she didn't respond to it.

Around four a.m. a radioman from the coast guard's San Francisco division sent a message to *Itasca*. "Have you established contact with the plane yet?" he asked.

"[We've] heard her," replied Radioman Third Class Thomas O'Hare, "but don't know if she hears us."

Itasca went on sending and listening. Just before five a.m. they heard Earhart again. "Partly cloudy," she reported before her voice was once again lost in static.

The Way It Works

Before the invention of our modern-day GPSs (global positioning systems), one method by which airplanes found their way across long distances was by using a radio direction finder (DF). The DF operator simply rotated a loop antenna in search of radio signals being transmitted (sent) by the beacon (the broadcasting station).

These radio signals were strongest when the antenna loop was lined up with them. They were weakest when the side of the loop was ninety degrees away from them. Curiously, the weakest signals were the easiest to hear and were far more accurate. So the DF operator rotated his loop to find the weakest signal (called a null). He could then get a fix on the source of the transmission—it was always ninety degrees away from the null—and find his way.

DFs could pick up only certain radio frequencies. These frequencies had to be strong, and they had to last at least three minutes for the operator to home in on them. Despite these limitations, pilots relied heavily on them. They were, wrote one aviation columnist, "as unerring as a bird dog sniffing a quail-scented breeze."

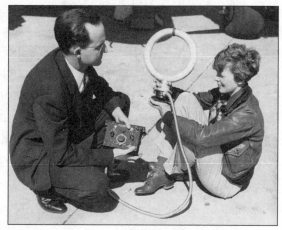

Amelia and her husband, George Putnam, examine the radio direction finder (DF) before it's installed on her plane. Note the loop antenna.

Tense, Bellarts leaned closer to his radio set. For more than an hour, he and the other radiomen heard only the scratching of empty air waves. Then—

6:14 a.m.: "*ITASCA*, THIS IS KHAQQ. . . . WANT BEARING. . . . WILL WHISTLE IN MIKE."

Earhart then announced she was about two hundred miles away and started whistling into her radio's microphone.

Itasca's crew was surprised. The ship did have a direction finder that could pick up radio signals and determine where they were coming from. But their finder was unable to pick up the radio frequency Earhart was broadcasting on. Now, as she whistled into her mike, they realized the horrible truth—they could not help her! Remembered Leo Bellarts, "I was sitting there sweating blood because I couldn't do a darn thing about it."

Then Earhart stopped transmitting. For thirty minutes, radio operators tried making contact with her. Then, suddenly, she was back on the air, stronger than ever.

6:45 a.m.: "PLEASE TAKE BEARING ON US. . . . I WILL MAKE NOISE IN MIKE. . . . ABOUT ONE HUNDRED MILES OUT."

What could *Itasca*'s crew do? For nearly an hour, radiomen frantically sent signals and messages, praying she could hear them. Crew members knew the plane had been aloft for nineteen hours now, and Earhart's fuel was running low. Along the ship's deck and on Howland Island itself, sailors gazed upward, their ears straining for the distant rumble of plane engines. "It was past dawn and the sky was partly cloudy," remembered one crew member. "The *Itasca* . . . [sent] out huge clouds of smoke while we lined the runway and sat out in lifeboats and the official greeters waited anxiously at the reception spot. All eyes gazed fondly, proudly, eagerly over the horizon. We believed we were about to see history in the making—the first woman to fly around the world, but she didn't come, and she didn't come."

And then her voice broke through the static.

7:42 a.m.: "WE MUST BE ON YOU, BUT CANNOT SEE YOU. GAS IS RUNNING LOW. BEEN UNABLE TO REACH YOU BY RADIO. WE ARE FLYING AT AN ALTITUDE OF 1,000 FEET."

Earhart's radio signal was so strong, Bellarts believed she had to be directly overhead. He stepped out of the radio room and listened, convinced he would hear a plane motor any second. He didn't.

7:58 a.m.: "KHAQQ CALLING *ITASCA*. WE ARE LISTENING BUT CANNOT HEAR YOU. . . ."

Bellarts knew this meant trouble. By now Earhart should have reached the island. But obviously she could see neither Howland nor the ship with its billowing smoke. This could mean only one thing—Amelia Earhart was lost.

8:00 a.m.: "KHAQQ CALLING *ITASCA*. WE RECEIVED YOUR SIGNALS BUT UNABLE TO GET A MINIMUM. PLEASE TAKE BEARING ON US AND ANSWER ON 3105. . . ."

Bellarts now knew with certainty that there was something wrong with Earhart's radio. She still did not know that they could not get a bearing on 3105 kilocycles.

All they could do was go on sending radio signals. "We were trying everything," Bellarts later said. "We tried stuff that actually is not in the log. . . . Really, I mean it. We was frantic."

Then—forty-five anxious minutes later—she was back:

8:45 a.m.: "WE ARE ON LINE 157-337. WE WILL REPEAT MESSAGE. . . . WE ARE RUNNING ON LINE NORTH AND SOUTH."

The fear in Earhart's voice made Leo Bellarts's skin prickle. "I'm telling you, it sounded as if she would have broken out in a scream. . . . She was just about ready to break into tears and go into hysterics. . . . I'll never forget it."

Seconds turned to minutes. Minutes became an hour. But the sky above Howland Island remained empty.

And in the radio room, Leo Bellarts and the other crew members sat listening to the "mournful sound of that static."

Where, they wondered, was Amelia Earhart?

Little Amelia

1897 to 1908

LOOKING BACK ON HER CHILDHOOD, Amelia Earhart claimed she could see "certain threads . . . leading me to airplanes."

There was the thread "of liking all kinds of sports and games and not being afraid to try those that, back then, were looked upon as being only for boys."

There was the thread of "liking to experiment and of something inside me that always liked to try new things."

And there were other threads, too, "weaving in and out and here and there through the years before airplanes and I got together."

But as Amelia liked to say, "It is best to begin at the beginning."

BABY EARHART

Amelia Mary Earhart was born in her grandparents' house in Atchison, Kansas, on July 24, 1897. Her father, Edwin, was a lawyer who represented several railroad companies—a job that often took him away from home. Her mother, Amy, was the indulged daughter of a prominent Kansas judge. Both Edwin and Amy adored their little girl, and for the first three years of Amelia's life, they lived happily together in an ordinary white frame house in Kansas City, about fifty miles from Atchison.

"Baby Earhart sleeps all the time," Amy recorded in her baby book. She "never sucks her thumb like other infants," and by twelve weeks she could "laugh and talk to herself in the looking glass." By May little Amelia was crawling, and three months later she took her first step. "Highly independent and precocious—that's our baby," her mother wrote proudly.

Edwin and Amy Earhart on their wedding day.

After Amelia's second birthday, Amy recorded, "Baby goes to bed by herself, often singing herself to sleep." Amelia was "highly imaginative" and would "amuse herself for hours with imaginary friends."

"Even then," her mother would later claim, "Amelia had a strong, self-sufficient streak."

LIFE IN ATCHISON

At the age of three, Amelia was bundled off to live with her grandmother Otis (her mother's mother) in Atchison. "I was lent to her for company during the winter months," Amelia later explained.

The first picture ever taken of Amelia, October 1897.

No one in the family seemed to think this was an unusual arrangement. Amelia's grandmother desperately needed distraction from the recent deaths of her eldest son and his wife from diphtheria. And Amelia's mother had her hands full with a new baby (sister Muriel had been born in December 1900). Sending Amelia to Atchison seemed the perfect way to lighten Amy's workload as well as lift Grandmother Otis's spirits.

The Otis house in Atchison, Kansas, where Amelia spent much of her childhood.

Amelia at age three holding her sister, Muriel. This picture was taken around the time Amelia was sent to live with her grandmother.

Grandmother Otis with Amelia.

Grandmother Otis was in her sixties when Amelia arrived. Her greatest interests were her family, her flower gardens and her church. Now, with little Amelia at her side, she puttered happily about the kitchen, baking cookies. On warm spring days, she picnicked with the child in the sunken garden and played hide-and-seek with her in the apple orchard. She gave Amelia the best bedroom in the house—the one with a huge window overlooking the Missouri River—and she let her decorate it any way she chose.

"It was a happy existence," recalled Amelia. The only problem was Grandmother Otis's insistence on ladylike behavior. She fussed if Amelia got her clothes dirty and often corrected her table manners. But Grandmother Otis was especially particular about "ladylike deportment."

One day, Grandmother Otis caught six-year-old Amelia jumping over the wrought-iron fence that surrounded the house.

"Ladies don't climb fences," admonished Grandmother Otis. "Only boys do that. Little girls use the gate."

Amelia was puzzled. She felt sure that if she had been a boy, her grandmother would have thought the shortcut "entirely natural." "The rules of female conduct," she later said, "bewildered and annoyed [me]."

In Atchison, Amelia's best friends were Lucy and Kathryn (Toot and Katch) Challis and Virginia Park, nicknamed Ginger. The four girls—Millie (as Amelia was called), Ginger, Toot and Katch—were inseparable. "Millie was always the instigator," recalled Toot. "She would dare anything, and we would all follow along." Added Katch, "I just adored her. . . . She was not only fun . . . she could do *everything*."

Millie led this little band of girls in mud-ball fights, on picnics and on explorations along the bluffs of the Missouri River. They roller-skated, rode bikes and played endless innings of baseball. But their favorite pastime was a made-up game called Bogie. "It was played in my grandmother's barn and consisted of taking imaginary journeys to deepest Africa and darkest Asia in an old abandoned carriage," remembered Amelia.

Amelia used her vivid imagination to transform the old carriage into a camel or elephant or magic carpet. Equipped with toy pistols and hand-drawn maps, they crossed the Bridge of Skeletons, passed through the Witches' Cave and lost their way

Amelia at age six, looking very much the proper little girl.

Amelia (right) pictured with best friend "Toot" Challis.

in the Dark Woods. There were all sorts of other dangers, too—girl-eating lions, howling ghosts and "hairy men" who would have carried them away if Millie hadn't saved the day. Once, finding a forgotten gumdrop in her pocket, she heaved it at the villains. "The hairy men evaporated," recalled Ginger.

On snowy winter days, the friends liked to meet at the top of the North Second Street hill with their sleds. At that time, boys and girls rode different types. A girl's sled was like a little chair on wooden runners. The rider sat upright on the chair and coasted in a ladylike manner down the hill. But Amelia didn't want to coast. She wanted to soar. So she asked her father for a boy's sled—the flat kind with steel runners. "I wanted to use it for belly whoppers," she said. Much to Grandmother Otis's dismay, her father agreed. Amelia became the only girl in town who could lie down while sledding. "Tomboy," some of the prissier girls whispered. But Amelia shrugged off their insults. She was having "too marvelous of a time." Then one afternoon, as she zipped down the icy hill, a junkman's cart came out of a side road. She screamed a warning, but the junkman didn't hear her. Unable to stop, Amelia aimed for the space between the horse's front and back legs. Because she was lying down, she made it. "That tomboy method saved my life," she said.

SCHOOL DAYS

From first grade on, Amelia attended Atchison's College Preparatory School. It was a tiny place with only forty students, housed in a building that had once been a stable.

Amelia was one of just three first graders. "I can remember days when I was the only one in my class," she later wrote.

Amelia was a good student and excelled at reading. She devoured back issues of *Harper's Magazine for Young People* and the novels of Charles Dickens and Sir Walter Scott. On the crowded bookshelves in Grandmother Otis's library she also found some old children's books. Amelia turned up her nose at these. "They were all about very

Amelia Earhart, Poet

Besides reading, Amelia enjoyed writing poetry. She composed this verse when she was eight:
I watch the birds flying all day long,
And I want to fly too.
Don't they look down sometimes, I wonder,
And wish they were me,
When I'm going to the circus with my daddy?

good little boys and girls emerging triumphant over very bad little boys and girls," she recalled. "They reminded me of the dull sermons I was forced to sit through on Sunday mornings."

Instead, she preferred reading "western thrillers" and "medieval romances," and "often wondered why the girls in the books were not allowed to have the exciting adventures that boys did."

Besides being a strong reader, Amelia was excellent at math—even if she did refuse to show her work. "Why bother to write out the steps if I can deduce the answer in my head?" she asked. Wrote her obviously exasperated third-grade teacher, Miss Walton, "Amelia's mind is brilliant, but she listens to another drummer."

Amelia was good at sports, too. But she wasn't allowed to play on any of the school's teams. In those days, team sports were for

Amelia's report card, 1906–1907.

boys only. Girls were expected to simply be cheerleaders. This wasn't enough for Amelia. She wanted to learn the rules of basketball so she could play the game with her friends. So one day she appeared in the school gymnasium during basketball practice. Walking boldly up to team captain Frank Baker, she said, "We girls would like to play."

At first Frank was surprised. But eventually he agreed to teach Amelia how to hold the ball and shoot for the basket. Amelia immediately taught Ginger, Toot and Katch. Soon the girls were playing every afternoon in the park across the street (a single hoop had been mounted on the side of a barn). "I was fond of basketball,"

Amelia said later, "as well as bicycling and tennis, and I tried any and all strenuous games. . . . What intense pleasure exercise gave me!"

LIFE IN KANSAS CITY

At the start of every summer, Amelia returned to her parents and sister in Kansas City—a fifty-mile journey that took her from her grandmother's proper, well-ordered household to a simpler, less structured place. Her father especially believed in letting the girls do whatever they wanted, whether it was considered ladylike or not. He took Amelia and Muriel fishing. He let them stay up past midnight to see an eclipse of the moon. And he bought them toys most people would have considered appropriate only for boys.

"Dear Dad," Amelia once wrote. "Muriel and I would like footballs please. We need them specially as we have plenty of baseballs, bats, etc. . . ."

The footballs arrived, along with a .22 rifle. "Oh, now, don't worry, [Grandmother] Otis," Edwin wrote his fussing mother-in-law. "This is really a very small rifle." Amelia and Muriel used the rifle to shoot rats in the barn. "It was the biggest game either of us ever hunted," remembered Amelia.

In Kansas City, the Earhart girls' constant companion was their big black dog, James Ferocious. They were always harnessing him to a small cart, or decorating him with hair ribbons, or "mauling him affectionately." James happily endured it all. But while the dog adored his family, he was not very friendly toward strangers. For this reason, the Earharts tied him to the shed when they were away.

One afternoon, while the girls were taking naps, two neighbor boys wandered into the yard and began teasing the tied-up dog. "One boy would step into the circle of his chain, then, when James leaped at him, [the boy] would jump back to safety," said Muriel.

But the boys tried the trick once too often. James lunged. The chain broke. And the boys pulled themselves onto the roof of the shed, just barely escaping James's jaws. That was when Amelia—awakened by the dog's crazed barking—stepped into the backyard. She had never seen the dog behave so fiercely. Still, she said calmly,

Bloomers!

The summer Amelia turned eight, her mother had a seamstress make bloomers for both her daughters. The bloomers—dark blue flannel, full and pleated and gathered at the knees—freed the girls from the skirts they wore all day. "This was rare," remembered Muriel, "because [in those days] all nice little girls wore full-skirted dresses with ruffled pinafores over them." Twenty-five years later, Amelia remembered with "special glee" putting on her bloomers and heading outside "to shock all the nice little girls. It seems a trivial thing now, but it was tremendously daring in those strictly conventional days."

Muriel (on the swing) and Amelia wearing their bloomers.

"James Ferocious, you naughty dog, you've tipped over your water dish." Then she put her hand on his raised hackles and led him into the kitchen.

"How brave you were!" exclaimed her mother.

"I wasn't brave," replied Amelia. "I just didn't have time to be scared."

Amelia liked collecting things, and in her Kansas City bedroom she kept an assortment of animal bones, including a cow skull. She also collected moths, katydids and toads. This fascination with the natural world came from her mother. Once, Amy called the girls in to see how an earthworm moved without legs. Another time, while cutting up a chicken, she showed them how the lungs fit into the body, and how the wings were jointed like hands and wrists. "It was," admitted Amelia, "both educational and unusual."

WHAT A RIDE!

In the summer of 1905, the Earhart family traveled to the St. Louis World's Fair. Eight-year-old Amelia loved every minute of it—the exhibits, the animals, the ice cream. She rode the Ferris wheel with her father, then begged for a turn on the roller coaster. But her mother said no. "It is too dangerous for little girls."

Undaunted, Amelia returned to Atchison the following fall and decided to build her own roller coaster. Muriel, who had also been sent to Grandmother Otis's that fall, recalled how her sister found some wooden two-by-fours, propped them at an angle against the toolshed to make the track and built a cab out of a wooden crate and baby buggy wheels.

Kids from all over the neighborhood came to help, and soon the coaster was ready. Amelia went first. Swooshing down the steep incline, she hit the ground and somersaulted head over heels. She picked herself up. Ignoring her torn dress and bruised lip, she declared, "Oh . . . it's just like flying." Then, ever practical, she studied the coaster's design. "We need more track," she decided. After making the adjustment, she tried again. This time it worked. "A ride down that thing was a thrill," recalled a neighbor boy. Sadly, the coaster didn't last long. Grandmother Otis took one look at it and declared it dangerous. The roller coaster was taken down.

CHANGES

In 1908 Edwin Earhart took a job as a claims agent with the Chicago, Rock Island & Pacific railroad line. The job offered more money, but it also meant the Earharts would have to move to Des Moines, Iowa. Moving would mean changes for all of them, but most especially for eleven-year-old Amelia. It would be the end of living with Grandmother Otis; the end of playing with Toot, Katch and Ginger; the end of College Preparatory School. Little did Amelia know that it would also be the end of her happy childhood.

The DAY WEARS ON

ABOARD ITASCA, commanding officer Warner Thompson had a decision to make. Should he order the cutter to begin searching for Earhart right away, or should he wait? By his calculations, her plane had enough fuel to stay in the air for another hour or so. In that time she still might reestablish radio contact. She might even appear overhead.

And so *Itasca* waited. On deck, crew members shaded their eyes and peered into the blue sky, hoping for the glint of a plane wing. Meanwhile, in the radio room Leo Bellarts and the other operators desperately banged out Morse code messages. But the sky remained empty; the radio merely scratched and hissed.

Finally, at 1:45 p.m., Commander Thompson ordered Bellarts to send an all-emergency broadcast to "ALL SHIPS, ALL STATIONS: AMELIA EARHART PLANE . . . APPARENTLY DOWN AT SEA, POSITION UNKNOWN. . . . REQUEST SHIPS AND STATIONS LISTEN . . . FOR ANY SIGNALS FROM PLANE. . . ." Then he gave the command for *Itasca* to get under way. They would search the waters north and west of Howland Island. Explained Thompson, "The area seemed most logical" based on the position given by Amelia in her last broadcast.

As the cutter churned through the Pacific's swells, every set of available eyes scanned the ocean. Was it possible the plane could be floating—intact—on the water's surface? Or could Amelia be clinging to a piece of wreckage? Might she even have had time to inflate a life raft? But hour after tense hour passed without a sign of the flier.

Then miraculously, at six o'clock that evening, *Itasca's* radiomen heard a weak voice behind the static. Unfortunately, none of the men could make out any of the words.

The radio operators quickly sent a reply. "YOU ARE VERY WEAK. REPEAT. PLEASE GO AHEAD."

They waited.

No reply.

Minutes later they sent another message, and this time they tried something new. "PLEASE GIVE LONG DASHES [IN MORSE CODE] IF YOU HEAR US. GO AHEAD."

For several long seconds, only static filled the room. Then the voice was back. Wrote radioman Thomas O'Hare in the ship's log, "We hear her now. Very weak and unreadable voice."

Chief Radioman Leo Bellarts stepped in. "IF YOU HEAR US PLEASE GIVE US A SERIES OF LONG DASHES," he transmitted.

Bellarts got an immediate reply—an on-again-off-again signal he described in his log as "something like a generator start and stop."

It was not the reply they expected. Normally, dots and dashes were sent by simply holding down and releasing a "sending key." But what *Itasca*'s crew didn't know was that Amelia did not have a sending key on her airplane. To make dashes, she had to hold down and release the push-to-talk button on her radio microphone. Every time she did this, it sounded like a generator going on and off.

Could Amelia have been using her radio microphone to send a message?

Since the radiomen did not try to decipher it, no one will ever know.

Minutes later, the generator sound was repeated. This time, Bellarts thought he also heard someone say the name Earhart.

But was it really the aviator? The radiomen weren't sure. Wrote O'Hare in his log, "Signals on and off. Think it is the plane?"

Itasca called again in both voice and Morse code. This time a man's voice answered. A man? Crewmembers didn't know that Amelia had taken along a navigator named Fred Noonan. They believed she had attempted the journey alone. Hearing the man's voice made them think the signal was a hoax. Logged O'Hare, "Guess it isn't her now."

Morse Code: The Long and Short of It

Morse code is a way of communicating through telegraph lines, undersea cables and radio waves. Invented by Samuel F. B. Morse in the early 1840s, it uses a sequence of long and short sounds that represent the letters of the alphabet. Short tones are called dots; long tones are called dashes. A message in Morse code is sent by using a switch called a sending key to break the radio signal. The long and short tones between these breaks are then decoded into the letters of the alphabet, and the message is received.

A sending key similar to the one used by the radiomen of Itasca. Amelia did not have a key aboard her plane and would have had to use the on-off button on her microphone to break the radio signal.

Send a Secret Message in Morse Code

Of course, you don't need a radio signal or a telegraph key to send a message in Morse code. You and your friends can send each other top-secret dots-and-dashes messages simply by turning a flashlight on and off, tapping a pencil, or even batting your eyelids. Want to know more? Go to www.education.com/activity/article/Morse_Code and start signaling your friends today.

Letter	Code	Letter	Code
A	·—	N	—·
B	—···	O	———
C	—·—·	P	·——·
D	—··	Q	——·—
E	·	R	·—·
F	··—·	S	···
G	——·	T	—
H	····	U	··—
I	··	V	···—
J	·———	W	·——
K	—·—	X	—··—
L	·—··	Y	—·——
M	——	Z	——··

Fig. 82.—Morse alphabet.

This chart of the International Morse Code shows how letters and numbers are represented by dots and dashes.

Family Secret

1908 to 1916

"LIFE IN DES MOINES WAS MAGICAL . . . FOR A WHILE," said Muriel. The Earharts lived in four different houses in Des Moines, moving each year to a bigger and better home as Edwin's salary from the railroad increased. Finally they landed on Cottage Grove Street, in the most fashionable part of town. Their new affluence allowed them to hire a cook and a maid; to purchase season tickets to the symphony; to buy silk party dresses and fur-trimmed coats and a fine rosewood piano for the parlor.

That first fall in Iowa, Amelia entered the seventh grade. "I had a passion

The Earharts' big house on Cottage Grove Street in Des Moines.

for math and science," she remembered. She also "learned a bit about politics" when one teacher, Miss Pearl De Jarnette, ran for superintendent of the schools. This was highly unusual. Very few women held public office back then; at that time women weren't even allowed to vote. Still, Amelia flung herself into the campaign by making a big cardboard sign that read

DOWN WITH THE MAN! UP WITH THE LADY! On Election Day she carried it around and around the schoolyard. "She always claimed her happy parading won Miss De Jarnette the election," said Muriel.

Meanwhile, Edwin was doing so well in his new job that he was soon put in charge of the entire Rock Island claims department.

Amelia, Muriel, Edwin and Tokimo stand on the platform of their private railroad car.

One of the perks of his important new position was use of the company's private railroad car. It came complete with its own kitchen, its own dining room and Tokimo, a "superb" Japanese chef. "Bring the girls and Sadie [the maid] and meet me . . . ," Edwin would wire from wherever he was working. Then the four would climb aboard the luxurious car and chug off to St. Louis, or Minneapolis, or the Ozark Mountains.

DAD'S SICKNESS

For two short years the Earharts lived together happily. Then Edwin began to drink. He had enjoyed an occasional whiskey in the past, so it seemed like nothing at first—just a drink or two with friends after work. But the habit grew. Soon he was drinking at lunchtime . . . then all afternoon . . . then staggering home from work two or three times a week. His easygoing nature disappeared. "Dad brooded and raged," said Muriel. Still, the family managed to keep "Dad's sickness," as they called it, a secret.

Before he started drinking heavily, Edwin would come home from the office early on Saturdays to play cowboys and Indians with the neighborhood children.

"We'd whoop it up for an hour or two," recalled his younger daughter. "Afterward we gathered on the front steps of our house for . . . lemonade and cookies."

But one Saturday, as ten children eagerly waited on the front lawn, Edwin stumbled off the streetcar. He swayed down the street, and as he came closer, the children could smell whiskey on his clothes. "We escorted him to the door in a curious silence, and he lurched up the stairs," recalled Muriel. "Mother opened the door, and her face became frozen. She helped Dad inside, and closed the door behind him." In the yard, the Earhart girls' "cheeks blazed with embarrassment." The ugly truth was out. Soon the whole neighborhood knew about Edwin's drinking.

"In a twinkling, our magical life ended," Muriel said. Now each night the girls listened for their father's footsteps outside the house. A brisk step meant that a sober, loving Edwin was coming home; a shuffling pace meant the return of that angry, thick-tongued stranger who cursed and yelled. The once-playful girls stopped joking, because they never knew what might cause Edwin's temper to flare. Once when Amelia found a bottle of his whiskey and poured it out, Edwin raised his hand in anger. "I believe he would have struck her if Mother had not come running from the dining room and seized his arm from behind," said Muriel. If their father was home, the girls ate their dinner quickly, eager to get away from the table. And they spent most evenings locked away in their bedrooms.

As 1911 drew to a close, Grandmother Otis lay dying. Amy Earhart hurried to her mother's side, taking her daughters with her. The three remained in Atchison until the older woman's death in February 1912. How Amelia felt about losing such an important person in her life is not known. She never wrote about the event or confided her feelings to anyone. Amy Earhart, however, claimed that her daughter was "devastated."

Grandmother Otis left behind an estate worth half a million dollars (close to nine million dollars nowadays). Amy should have received a fourth of this money. But Grandmother Otis had heard about Edwin's drinking. Convinced he would squander the inheritance, she had changed her will just months before. Her new will specified that Amy's money be locked into a trust for fifteen years or until

Edwin's death. Worse, the *Atchison Globe* published the terms of the will for every-one to read. Now the whole town knew that Mrs. Otis considered her son-in-law a drunk.

The public humiliation drove Edwin to drink even more heavily. Soon he began making mistakes at work, filing inaccurate reports and overpaying claims. The head office noticed. They sent a manager to check on Edwin. When the manager arrived at the Des Moines office, he found Edwin drunk at his desk. He fired Edwin on the spot.

Desperate for work, Edwin wrote to railroad claim offices all over the country. But his dismissal for drinking had become common knowledge among the railroad companies. "No one wanted to hire a man who couldn't be trusted to stay sober," said Muriel.

The family lived on what little savings they had. They fired the maids, stopped buying dresses and quit going to the symphony. They hoped Edwin would find a job soon.

LEAN YEARS

An entire year passed before Edwin found another job—this time as a freight clerk for the Great Northern railway in St. Paul, Minnesota. It was a drop in status—a menial job—but the Earharts desperately needed the money. So in the spring of 1913, the family packed up and moved north. As the train pulled out of Des Moines, Amelia saw tears running down her mother's cheeks, and that night she heard thirteen-year-old Muriel praying:

"Forgive us our trespasses as we forgive those who trespass against us, except I'll never, never forgive saloon keepers, all of them, everywhere."

Life in St. Paul was cold and lonely. The Earharts rented a big, shabby house on Fairmont Street. Edwin did not make enough money to heat the place, so half the rooms had to be closed off.

The price of food strained the family budget, too. Sixteen-year-old Amelia took over the family marketing. To save pennies, she chose a cheap grocery store that

This photograph, taken in St. Paul, shows how worried-looking and thin sixteen-year-old Amelia had become.

was three miles from home. Even on the coldest days, she trudged through the snow. When Muriel asked why she didn't take the bus, Amelia replied, "I can save ten cents by walking."

Amelia had other money-saving ideas, too. One spring day, she emerged from the attic with "a pleased look on her face and a pair of old curtains in her arms." She immediately set about transforming those curtains into Easter outfits for herself and Muriel. First she dyed the curtains a deep shade of green. Then she sewed two lengths of the dyed material together to make a simple skirt, hemmed the bottom and added a belt to cinch in the waist. On Easter morning, as Muriel headed proudly off to church in her new outfit, Amelia warned, "If it should begin to rain, for heaven's sakes, get under shelter before you leave a trail of green dye on the sidewalk." Luckily, the weather was dry. Best of all, the sisters gained "a lesson in making do with cheerfulness."

Both girls attended Central High School—Amelia as a junior, Muriel as a freshman. The school taught a wide range of subjects, and Amelia took advantage of them. She enrolled in physics, Latin and German. Still, her favorite subject remained math. "She preferred algebra to geometry," recalled her mother, "because she had to work at geometry while she could do algebra in her head." Amelia was also "miles ahead" of the other juniors when it came to literature. "The things they read are so childish," she told her mother. "I don't believe they've ever heard of Shakespeare."

At first, Amelia did well, earning a grade average of ninety-one. But the strain of her home life obviously made studying difficult. As the school year went on, her grades dropped. By the last quarter, her average had slipped to seventy-five.

In December, two neighbor boys invited Amelia and Muriel to a Christmas dance. The girls were ecstatic. They had made few friends since moving to St. Paul and had not received a single party invitation—until now. Of course, in those days, the idea of teenagers going on a "date" did not exist. Instead, fathers were expected to escort their daughters to the dance and then pick them up afterward. Edwin promised to be home by six o'clock so he could take his daughters to the party.

That day, the girls decorated the living room because they had invited the boys over for cocoa and cookies after the dance. Then they put on their best party dresses and waited for their father. The clock ticked on through six . . . seven . . . eight o'clock.

Finally, at nine, Edwin staggered home drunk. Muriel burst into tears and ran up to her room. But not Amelia. She pulled down all the decorations, tore up the paper Christmas napkins and threw out the marshmallows that were already in the cups. Then she stormed up the stairs to her room. "Dad's broken trust was more painful than missing the dance," said Muriel.

SEPARATION

The following spring, in 1914, Edwin said he had been offered a job in the claims office of the Burlington railroad in Springfield, Missouri. Once again, the family packed up and moved on. But when they arrived at the Springfield train station, they learned the truth: There was no job. How could Edwin have made such an enormous mistake? His family believed it was because of his "sickness."

"Mother weighed her words carefully," remembered Muriel. "The three years of tension and humiliation through which we had just passed had been hard on all of us, and Mother had had enough. She told Father we were leaving him. . . . We would go to live with friends in Chicago."

Furious, Edwin called his wife hard-hearted and demanded she leave the girls behind. But Amy had made her decision. They headed for Chicago. As for Edwin, he returned to Kansas to live with his sister and open a new law practice.

These must have been painful years for Amelia, but she breezed over them later in her memoir, *The Fun of It*:

> The family rolled around a good deal during my father's railroad years, Kansas City, Des Moines, St. Paul, Chicago—forward and back. What we missed in continuous contacts over a long period, we gained by becoming adapted to new surroundings quickly. I have never lived more than four years in any one place and always have to ask, "Which one?" when a stranger greets me by saying "I'm from your home town."

In Chicago, seventeen-year-old Amelia attended Hyde Park High School. It was the best school in the city, offering advanced studies as well as dozens of clubs and activities. Ahead of its time, the school even had girls' basketball and baseball teams. But Amelia didn't take part in any of these activities. She had no friends and made no effort to fit in. The other students thought her strange. "Odd, different and a loner," remembered one classmate, "she spent most of her free time alone in the library." The yearbook's description of her summed up her loneliness. It read, "The girl in brown who walks alone."

The summer after graduation, Amelia's parents attempted to reconcile, and the family reunited in Kansas City. Edwin had stopped drinking and was practicing law. He had even rented a small house where they could all be together. But his illness had left its mark. Amelia still loved her father deeply, but she had also learned a hard lesson. "One really must rely on oneself," she said.

Nineteen-year-old Amelia longed to fly away—but to where?

MABEL'S STORY

AT THE EXACT TIME that *Itasca's* radiomen were trying to identify those generator sounds, Mabel Larremore was turning on her "very good shortwave set." Mabel, a homemaker in Amarillo, Texas, had finally tucked her two small sons into bed for the night. Now she looked forward to relaxing and listening to some overseas radio programs.

But as she turned the dial, she suddenly heard Amelia Earhart calling for help. Mabel knew it was Amelia, having heard the aviator's voice dozens of times before in radio interviews and in newsreels. And since Mabel's radio signal was "very clear," she had no trouble hearing Earhart's message.

Radio 101

Before the invention of television, Americans gathered around the radio to listen to music, newscasts, dramas and comedy programs. These shows were broadcast from nearby AM stations and were the most common form of entertainment in the 1930s.

Many radios also included a second dial for the shortwave radio. The shortwave radio differed from the regular AM one. While the AM radio could pick up only low-frequency radio signals sent from nearby stations, the shortwave radio could pick up high-frequency signals. Because these high-frequency signals could travel long distances, listeners never knew what they might hear simply by turning the shortwave dial (signals were random, depending on variables such as the weather and the time of day). They might pick up a signal from Hawaii or Italy or even faraway Russia. Back in the 1930s, this was a common (and exciting) way to stay in touch with the rest of the world.

This radio, manufactured by Philco in 1937, was typical of those found in homes across the United States. The shortwave radio dial is in the center of the console.

"Her message stated that the plane was down on an uncharted island," Mabel later told the *Amarillo Globe News*. "[It] was partially on land, part in water. She gave the latitude and longitude of her location." According to Mabel, Amelia also stated that her navigator, Fred Noonan, was seriously injured and needed a doctor. She, too, was hurt, but not as badly. "I listened to her for thirty or forty minutes after waking my family to listen," recalled Mabel. But she didn't contact any officials because she assumed "the government of the USA was taking care of everything."

Was Mabel's story true?

Could Amelia Earhart really be calling for help?

Finding Herself

1916 to 1920

USING A PORTION OF HER MOTHER'S INHERITANCE (during their time in Chicago, Amy had gone to court to have her money released), nineteen-year-old Amelia headed off to Rydal, Pennsylvania, where she attended the Ogontz School. Ogontz was one of the best college-preparatory schools in the country, offering classes in everything from French cooking to fencing. There were guest lecturers, trips to art museums in New York City and Washington, D.C., and even dancing lessons.

Amelia flung herself into everything. As she wrote to her mother:

> Weekdays this is the program.
> 7:00 Get up to a cow bell.
> 7:30 Prayers and afterward . . . exercises.
> 8:00 Breakfast and a morning walk till school begins at nine.
> Classes until two . . . Then, [field] hockey, [basket] ball . . . with an
> hour or two for tennis.
> 4–5:30 Study Hall
> 5:30–6:30 Dress for dinner

5:30–6:30 Dinner and prayers immediately after. Then spelling. Then every evening we have something to do. Thursday and Tuesday conversation classes in French or German etc. Wednesday a lecture or something like that . . . and Friday always something else. Saturday and Monday are our free nights. . . . Then everybody takes two hours of exercise out-doors. . . . You see every minute is accounted for and you have to go by the schedule.

Besides studying, Amelia also began to think seriously about her future. Even though the school's curriculum was rigorous and included subjects like chemistry, astronomy and logic, its administrators still believed that marriage was "the ideal vocation for women." Amelia did not agree. She began clipping newspaper and magazine articles about women who had careers, then pasted them into a scrapbook she called "Activities of Women." Among the women she singled out were a film producer, a police commissioner, an ocean liner captain and even a fire lookout for the Federal Forestry Service. "Such free and fascinating lives they must live," she wrote on the scrapbook's last page.

FIRST URGE TO FLY

During Christmas break in 1917, Amelia visited Muriel, who was attending school in Toronto. At that time, Canadians had been embroiled in what was later called World War I for more than three years (the United States had entered the war just months earlier). Amelia was shocked by the sight of so many wounded men on the streets and in city parks. Up to now she had been sheltered at school, "where the most pressing issue was what color sweater to wear." But seeing men without arms and legs, some blind, some on crutches, forced her to make a decision. "Returning to school was impossible with so much work to do," she said.

So she dropped out of Ogontz and stayed in Toronto. For the next year—until the end of the war in November 1918—Amelia worked as a volunteer nurse's aide. She made beds, delivered meal trays, emptied bedpans—"anything and everything to bring a little merry sunshine to the wounded men."

When she wasn't working at the hospital, Amelia often went horseback riding at the edge of the city near the Canadian Flying School. She found herself stopping again and again to watch the air force planes land and take off. "Beautiful and thrilling," said Amelia, "they were full-sized birds that slid on the hard-packed snow and rose into the air with an extra roar that echoed from the evergreens that banked the edge of the field." Moving close to them—so close the propellers threw snow into her face—she suddenly felt "a first urge to fly."

She tried to get permission to go up but failed. "Not even a general's wife could," recalled Amelia. So she did "the next best thing." She got to know the fliers.

And as she listened to their exciting stories of bad weather and air battles, "my imagination soared . . . as high as their aircraft," she said.

One afternoon, Amelia and a friend went to the Toronto fair to watch an exhibition of stunt flying. Wanting a better view of the action, they moved to the middle of the field. Amelia would never forget what happened next:

> The [pilot] was bored. He looped and rolled and spun and finished his little bag of tricks and there was nothing left to do

Amelia in her nurse's aide uniform in Toronto.

Planes like the kind Amelia saw at the Canadian Flying School.

Flight has long fascinated mankind. And over the centuries countless flying machines have been designed and built in hopes that people could take to the air. The first to get off the ground were the Montgolfier brothers in 1783. They created the first hot-air balloon and flew it over the city of Paris.

The next major advance came in 1845, when an Englishman, Sir George Cayley, designed a simple wooden glider with wings constructed of a lightweight fabric. Launched from the tops of hills, it stayed in the air for several minutes, but was also at the mercy of any strong gust of wind.

The dream of conquering the skies was not realized until the end of the nineteenth century. That was when two things happened: the lightweight, gas-driven internal-combustion engine was invented, and Wilbur and Orville Wright became fascinated with flight.

Wilbur and Orville Wright were bicycle salesmen from Dayton, Ohio, who were "afflicted with the belief that flight was possible." In the workroom behind their shop, they designed and invented.

What did they create? The *Flyer*, a skeletal flying machine made of spruce, ash and muslin, with a wingspan of just 40 feet (today's Boeing 747 has a wingspan of 220 feet). It was powered by a tiny gas engine and two propellers and was controlled by a simple pulley system.

On December 17, 1903, with Orville at the controls, the *Flyer* shakily lifted off from Kitty Hawk, North Carolina, and flew 120 feet. "The airplane," reported one newspaper, "has arrived. No more is mankind tethered to earth." But airplanes were still rudimentary. Over the next several years, the Wright brothers improved their invention.

Here are just a few of aviation's early milestones:

1904—The Wright brothers' *Flyer II* becomes the first plane to maintain a flight longer than five minutes.

1909—The United States government buys its first airplane, a Wright brothers biplane. The Wrights begin teaching army officers how to fly at a specially built airstrip in College Park, Maryland.

1911— The Wrights' *Vin Fiz* (named after a brand of grape soda) becomes the first plane to fly across the United States. It takes eighty-four days and seventy stops, and it crashes so often that little of the original material is still on the plane when it arrives in California.

1912— The first plane armed with a machine gun is flown.

1914— The Aviation Section of the Signal Corps (part of the army) is established—the forerunner of our modern-day United States Air Force.

First flight—Orville Wright mans the Flyer, December 17, 1903.

but watch the people on the ground running as he swooped close to them. That's when he saw us in the clearing. He dove. I remember the mingled fear and pleasure that surged over me as I watched that small plane at the top of its earthward swoop. . . . I did not understand it at the time, but I believe that little red airplane said something to me as it swished by.

With a shriek, her friend ran off. But Amelia waved her hands in delight.

BACK IN THE STATES

When the war ended, Amelia headed to Columbia University in New York City. Her time in Toronto had left her with "a yen for medicine," and she enrolled in pre-med classes. But for reasons she never explained, she soon changed her mind. "It took me only a few months to discover I would not make an ideal physician," she wrote.

Perhaps it was because her parents—who had recently moved to Los Angeles— were "pleading" with her to come live with them. So, as she explained, "I yielded to their demands and headed to California for the summer of 1920 with the full intention of returning to Columbia in the fall."

But something happened in California that changed her life forever.

Said Amelia, "Aviation caught me."

AN UNUSUAL OFFER

WORD OF AMELIA'S DISAPPEARANCE soon became world news, and as the second day of the search for her dawned, a Hawaiian radio station made an unusual offer. Would the coast guard allow the radio station to broadcast a message to Amelia in hopes she could hear it?

The coast guard quickly agreed. Arrangements for the special broadcast were made with NBC's Hawaiian affiliate, KGU, and with Honolulu's other big commercial station, KGMB. Since Amelia was known to listen to both stations, broadcasters believed she might be tuned in for news of the search effort.

World headlines screamed the news of Amelia's disappearance.

While the radio stations sent their messages, coast guard and navy stations in Hawaii, and on Midway and Wake islands, planned to monitor the airwaves for any reply. Using their direction finders, they would try to determine where any answering signals were coming from.

By sundown, everyone—coast guard, navy and radio station—was ready. Across the central Pacific, radiomen hunkered down next to their radios.

Would Amelia call?

First Flight

1920 to 1927

AMELIA WENT TO HER FIRST AIR MEET just days after arriving in California. Flying was all the rage on the West Coast, and new airfields were opening almost every week.

There were twenty of them in the Los Angeles area alone, and there was always something going on there—plane races, stunt flying, wing walking.

"I remember that first meet," Amelia wrote years later. "The sky was blue and the flying conditions were perfect. . . . The planes streaked overhead like silver birds, gleaming in the sunlight."

Amelia turned to her father, who had come along with her. "Dad, you know, I think I'd like to fly."

Danger!

It wasn't safe to fly an airplane in 1920. Things always went wrong. "Never forget that the engine may stop in mid-air," read one pilots' manual. "At all times keep this in mind."

In May of that year, the United States Post Office hired the first forty pilots ever to deliver airmail. By year's end, fifteen of those pilots had died in crashes caused by faulty motors. "In those days the motor was not what it is today," wrote one pilot. "It would drop out without warning . . . and one would simply throw in one's hand; there was no hope of salvation."

But the danger was part of flying's magic in those days. The narrow escapes and near misses made the sport daring and exciting. "The danger," admitted Amelia, "made it all the more thrilling."

Edwin was not enthusiastic about the idea. But she dragged him under the rope that bordered the field for a closer look at the planes. She had dozens of questions. But suddenly she felt too shy to ask them herself.

"Dad," she said, pointing to a young man in uniform, "ask that officer how long it takes to [learn to] fly."

Edwin dutifully headed off to speak with the pilot and soon returned with the answer. "The average seems to be from five to ten hours."

Amelia just nodded, but "in her bones," she felt that "a [flight] would come soon."

She was right. The very next day, she returned to the airfield because Edwin had arranged a trial flight. "I am sure he thought one ride would be enough for me," she later wrote, "and he might as well act to cure me promptly."

A pilot stepped forward and shook their hands. "A good day to go up," he said pleasantly. Then he pointed to another flier. "He'll go up with us."

"Why?" asked Amelia.

The pilots exchanged grins. "I understood instantly," she said. "I was a girl—a nervous lady. I might jump out. There needed to be somebody to grab my ankles as I went over." She told the fliers she wasn't afraid, but they refused to listen. "I was not allowed to sit alone in the front cockpit."

None of that mattered once the plane left the runway. "I was surprised to be able to see the ocean after a few moments of climbing . . . then the Hollywood Hills seemed to peep over the edge of the cockpit . . . and I knew what I wanted to do with my life. . . . I knew I myself had to fly."

"I think I'd like to learn to fly," Amelia told her family that evening. She tried to sound casual, "knowing full well I'd die if I didn't."

"Not a bad idea," replied Edwin, just as casually. "When do you start?"

Amelia wasn't sure. She needed to do a bit of investigating first. "I told him I'd let him know shortly."

Edwin nodded, seemingly unconcerned. "I hadn't thought she actually meant it," he later said. So days later, when he learned she had signed up for lessons, he was surprised. In hopes of putting her off the idea, he told her he couldn't afford them. But Amelia was determined. She found a job in the mailroom of the local telephone company to pay for the lessons herself. What could Edwin do? "I let her fly," he said.

FLEDGLING FLIER

Amelia decided to take flying lessons at Kinner Field, where there was a female pilot. "I felt I should be less self-conscious taking lessons [from a woman]," she said.

Who was that woman?

Twenty-four-year-old Neta Snook, the only female flier in Southern California, who was in the business of carrying passengers and giving lessons.

Neta would never forget the first time she laid eyes on Amelia. She had just finished a long day of flying sightseers over Los Angeles when she noticed a white-gloved young woman heading her way. "More silly people with silly questions," thought Neta.

Amelia's Teacher

Only five feet tall, Neta Snook had a personality as bright as her red hair. As a child she was fascinated by airplanes, and later she took any job she could to pay for her flying lessons. Unable to bulldoze her way into the United States Air Force when war broke out in 1917 (she was rejected because she was a woman), she accepted a job as an airplane mechanic. After the war, she bought a wrecked Canuck (seen behind her) and rebuilt its engine. She loaded the plane onto a truck, drove it to a nearby pasture, assembled it and took off. She barnstormed her way across the country, charging passengers fifteen dollars for a fifteen-minute ride. After arriving in Los Angeles, she started her own business at Kinner Field, flying passengers, doing aerial advertising and teaching would-be fliers.

Neta Snook posing with her Canuck.

A Short Cut

One Saturday morning, as Amelia walked to the airfield (in order to save the bus fare), a friendly motorist and his small daughter offered her a ride.

"What do you do?" asked the little girl as they bumped along the road.

"I am learning to be a pilot," replied Amelia.

The little girl looked their passenger up and down. "But you don't look like an aviatrix," she finally said. "You have long hair."

The girl's words gave Amelia an idea. That night she began cutting her hair—a little each evening so as not to shock her mother—until it was short. After that, Amelia carefully curled her blond bob, creating such a natural, tousled look that no one thought she ever touched it. This hairdo, which she wore for the rest of her life, became part of her signature look.

This rare photograph shows the student Amelia in the front cockpit of Neta Snook's dual-control Canuck.

But the young woman was anything but silly. "I'm Amelia Earhart," she said in a straightforward manner, "and I want to learn to fly. Will you teach me?"

Yes, Neta replied, for a dollar a minute, and she expected to be paid after each lesson.

Amelia blanched. She didn't have that much money. Would Neta agree to monthly payments?

Neta would. From then on, recalled Amelia, "I began hopping about on credit with her."

On the day of Amelia's first lesson—January 3, 1921—she arrived at the airfield wearing khaki pants and boots along with a colorful scarf tied jauntily around her neck. "I began dressing the part of the pilot," she admitted. She even bought herself a knee-length leather jacket, which she slept in for several nights to give it a used look. Always the student, she also had a book about aerodynamics tucked under her arm. "I soon became accustomed to seeing her with a book," recalled Neta. "She always carried one."

Neta began the lesson by briefly explaining the basics of flight. Then, after tossing a helmet and a pair of goggles at Amelia, she told her to climb into the front cockpit of the rebuilt World War I Canuck that Neta had bought surplus.

A Few Flying Lessons from Amelia

Amelia gave this advice to would-be fliers in her 1932 book, *The Fun of It:*

One of the first things a student learns in flying is that he turns by pushing a rudder bar the way he wants to go. When he turns, he must bank or tip the wings at the same time. Why? Because if he doesn't, the plane will skid in exactly the same way a car does when it whirls too fast around a level corner.

The stick, as the name implies, extends from the floor of the cockpit. It is a lever by means of which the pilot can push the nose of the plane up or down. It also tips the wings. By pushing it to the left, the left wing is depressed, and vice versa.

The rudder bar, upon which one's feet rest, simply turns the nose of the ship left or right, a movement to be coordinated with the action of the stick. Today, by the way, especially in larger planes, a wheel much like the steering wheel of a car is used instead of the simple stick.

In addition to the stick and the rudder, the novice must be familiar with certain instruments placed before his eyes. . . . These instruments include a compass for direction, as well as others that show speed through the air, height above ground, revolutions per minute of the motor, and pressure and temperature of oil.

Once the student learns the basics of keeping the plane level, turning and landing, he is taught the fundamental stunts. These are of slips, stalls, and spins. . . . What are their average uses? Well, side slips sometimes come in handy in landing in a short field; stalls and spins in knowing what to avoid in normal flying. A vertical bank is necessary in very short turns, and loops and barrel rolls and their relatives and friends are mostly for fun.

Stunting may be an art if perfected and practiced by those who have the talent. . . . It should be understood that this precision flying is like tightrope walking—it only looks easy.

Amelia then included two pages of maneuvers that explained exactly how each stunt was performed.

The Canuck had two open cockpits. In each was a matching set of controls consisting of a rudder bar and a stick. As the instructor, Neta sat in the back cockpit. Amelia, who sat in the front seat, then duplicated whatever she did in the way of steering. Since the controls in the front cockpit were connected to those in the back, the teacher could quickly correct any mistake made by the student.

During her first lesson, Amelia merely learned to taxi. But by February, she had logged four hours in the air. "She was wholly confident," recalled Neta. "She would just take over and do it."

But confidence could not replace skill, and Amelia made lots of mistakes. "Why do you persist in leveling off so high above the ground?" Neta asked one day in

May about Amelia's landing. "I had to shove the plane's nose down. . . . Didn't you notice?"

Amelia shook her head. "I guess I was just daydreaming," she replied.

"Her in-flight daydreaming distressed me," Neta said later. "A good pilot's mind should be focused on flying. I decided then that for all her training, she was still very much a beginner."

The "beginner" made other, more dangerous mistakes. One day during an instruction flight, Amelia suddenly turned the plane toward Long Beach, some sixty miles away. Neta knew immediately where her student was headed, and she doubted the plane could make that long a flight unless the fuel tanks had been topped off. Cutting the plane's throttle, she yelled, "Did you check [the fuel] personally?"

Amelia shook her head. "Mr. Kinner [owner of the airfield] always keeps it full."

Neta paled. Good pilots, she knew, always checked their own fuel level. Fearing that she would soon hear the plane sputtering, out of gas, Neta took the controls and grimly turned the plane around.

When they landed back at the airfield, a relieved Bert Kinner hurried out to the runway. He told them the plane was almost on empty. "I didn't fill it last night because the fuel tanker never arrived," he explained.

Neta was furious. "Not for the first time, I wondered if I had misjudged her ability."

Even when Amelia wasn't flying, there was always something to do at the airstrip. Hangars needed to be cleaned. Planes needed to be repaired. Recalled Amelia, "We shellacked the canvas wings and

Neta Snook and Amelia in front of the Kinner Airster— "the prettiest plane I [have] ever seen," Amelia gushed. As for Neta, she claimed the Airster "didn't have any stability."

replaced struts . . . and when there was enough gasoline . . . took turns cruising over the bay." When there wasn't enough gas (and their work was all done), the airfield crowd huddled in the shade of the tin-roofed office to "talk airplanes." Occasionally, recalled Amelia, a plane landed, "causing clouds of dust on the dirt runway."

After only six months of flying lessons, Amelia decided "life would be incomplete unless I owned my own plane." The one she wanted was small, fast and painted bright yellow. Built by airstrip owner Bert Kinner, it took off more quickly, climbed more steeply and was faster and easier to handle than Neta's Canuck.

But Neta was worried. "That plane flew like a leaf," she recalled. It was much too difficult for an inexperienced flier to control.

Amelia's mind, however, was made up. She offered Bert Kinner the little bit of money she had saved by working at the telephone company. "I was still a long way from wiping out the balance owed of $2000 though," she admitted. So she borrowed all her sister's savings, and her mother gave her the rest. As for Edwin Earhart, he opposed the purchase. Still, "it was our money to do with as we wished," recalled Muriel, "and we wished to give Amelia wings."

Just before her twenty-fourth birthday, in July 1921, Amelia climbed into her brand-new Kinner Canary (named because of its color) and took the controls. Neta—who had volunteered to teach Amelia to fly the plane for free—was also along. But immediately on takeoff the plane's third cylinder failed. Desperately, Amelia tried to pull up over a stand of trees, but she pulled up too fast. The plane crashed into the trees, breaking its undercarriage and propeller.

Neta crawled out of the wreckage, hoping against hope that Amelia wasn't hurt.

She wasn't. She was standing next to the plane, grinning and powdering her nose. "We have to look nice [if] reporters arrive," she said.

"Even in those early years, Amelia understood the importance of publicity and of looking good," Neta later wrote.

Once the plane had been fixed, Amelia changed instructors, and Neta faded out of the picture. Amelia's new teacher, an ex–army pilot named John Montijo, taught her stunt flying—dives, tailspins, loops and barrel rolls. These tricks, Amelia admitted, were not so useful. "I learned them," she said, "mostly for fun."

Amelia's license from the Fédération Aéronautique Internationale.

In December of that year, Amelia took the flying test for a National Aeronautic Association license. It wasn't her finest flight. "One of the shock absorbers broke causing the wing to sag just as I was leaving the ground," she admitted. "I also made a thoroughly rotten landing." Still, her performance was good enough to pass.

Now she began appearing on the exhibition circuit, doing stunt flying. She didn't enjoy it. "I felt like a clown," she confessed. What she really wanted was to be "alone and aloft." But airplanes were expensive to take care of, and exhibitions provided the money for fuel and repairs.

Soon her name began to appear regularly in the local papers, with headlines such as:

PACIFIC COAST LADIES' DERBY, AN EXHIBITION
BY MISS AMELIA EARHART!

A LADY'S PLANE AS WELL AS A MAN'S—READ WHAT MISS EARHART
HAS TO SAY ABOUT A KINNER AIRSTER.

AIR STUDENT—AVIATRIX TO "DROP IN" FOR STUDY

"I don't crave publicity," Amelia told one reporter.

But, corrected her sister, Muriel, she "never objected to it."

By October 1922, Amelia felt so confident in her flying skills that she decided to see how high her plane could climb. While at an air meet at Rogers Field outside Los Angeles, she took off in her Kinner Canary and winged out of sight. "It was a good day," she later wrote, "and I climbed easily for about 13,000 feet. Then I began to have trouble . . . a terrific vibration and knocking started. There wasn't anything to do but come down, although I was still climbing fifty feet a minute."

Once she was back on the ground, officials read the plane's sealed barograph (an instrument that records altitude). She had climbed to 14,000 feet, setting a new women's altitude record.

The following spring, she took and passed the flight test to receive a license from the Fédération Aéronautique Internationale, an international aviation organization. She was only the sixteenth woman in the world to receive one.

Amelia Earhart was making a name for herself.

GROUNDED

But family demands soon grounded her. Her parents (whose relationship had remained rocky even after Edwin had stopped drinking) were divorced in the summer of 1924. Amelia agreed to travel east with her mother to Boston, where Muriel was now studying. Selling her beloved plane, Amelia bought a sporty yellow car for the trip. Then mother and daughter headed east. "I still didn't think of my flying as a means to anything but having fun," Amelia admitted, "so I was not entirely devastated."

But what could she do to make a living?

Once again she considered medical school. Leaving her mother in Boston, Amelia returned to Columbia University. She took a few courses—physics and algebra—but school no longer inspired her. By the summer of 1925 she was back in Boston and looking for work. Her search brought her to Denison House.

Denison House, one of the oldest settlement houses in the country, helped new immigrants by providing food, medical care and English classes. Amelia had no background in social work. She was simply looking for a part-time job. But head worker Marion Perkins liked "her personality and confidence in herself so much that I gave her a position . . . without asking much about her training."

A Little Romance

While living in California, the Earharts took in boarders to help make ends meet. One of them was a tall, dark engineering student named Sam Chapman. He and Amelia soon began playing tennis together, going to the theater and spending evenings at home discussing books.

Sam was obviously more serious about the relationship than Amelia. He followed her east when she moved to Boston in 1924, and he repeatedly begged her to marry him. Amelia eventually agreed.

But did she ever really intend to marry him? Probably not.

Marriage, she said, was like "living the life of a domestic robot." "I don't want to marry Sam," she confided to her sister. "I don't want to marry anyone."

What did she want?

"To do what makes me happiest," she declared, "no matter what other people say."

Still, they were engaged until 1928, when Amelia finally broke it off. Sam would remain a close friend for the rest of her life.

Sam Chapman (far right) and Amelia (second from right), photographed on the Earharts' sofa in 1922, had a comfortable relationship. Kind and considerate, Sam was deeply in love with Amelia. He patiently waited (for years!) for her to give up her career plans and settle down to a traditional life as wife and mother.
She never did.

Amelia loved every busy minute of her days at Denison House. She formed girls' clubs, arranged music lessons, taught English and even created a girls' basketball team. "The 1926 season was fine," wrote Amelia, "having taken on and beaten a New York City team from Greenwich Settlement House."

She still yearned to fly, but she did not earn enough at Denison House to buy another airplane. Instead, she made friends with local pilots and joined the Boston chapter of the National Aeronautic Association.

In September of 1927, Amelia went to a nearby airstrip to watch the leading woman stunt flyer, Thea Rasche, demonstrate her skills. But during her performance, Rasche's engine conked out. The aviatrix tried to restart the engine, but the motor was dead. So Rasche put the plane into a glide, crashing into a swamp next to the runway. Rasche was shaken but uninjured.

"See?" some people in the crowd grumbled. "Women shouldn't be allowed to fly."

"They can't handle mechanical equipment," said others.

Their comments infuriated Amelia. "I decided I would show them," she said. Racing to the hangar, she hopped into one of the field's Waco 10s and amazed the crowd with what a newspaper later called "an excellent demonstration of flying." She looped the loop, pitched and rolled.

Why had she done it?

"Miss Earhart wanted to prove that . . . women are quite as capable pilots as men, and quite as daring," the *Boston Globe* reported. She had also put herself in the public eye.

Not long afterward, the telephone at Denison House rang.

"I'm too busy to answer just now,"

The children of Denison House surround Amelia at the wheel of the sporty yellow car she had bought in 1924.

Amelia said when she was told the call was for her. "Ask whoever it is to call again later."

"But he says it's important," insisted the messenger.

Grudgingly, Amelia went to the phone.

"You don't know me," said the man's voice on the other end, but "would you be interested in doing something for aviation which might be dangerous?"

What was this hazardous undertaking? Amelia asked.

But the man refused to tell her . . . yet.

VOICES *in the* NIGHT

AT SUNDOWN, sailors on Howland Island huddled next to their radios. They had been instructed to "listen continuously" for any signals from Earhart's plane.

On nearby Baker Island, radio operator Paul Yat Lum also listened for signals.

And aboard *Itasca*, Chief Radioman Leo Bellarts and Radioman Third Class George Thompson took the watch. If Amelia responded to the NBC station broadcast in Honolulu, they wanted to be the ones to hear it.

They weren't the only ones listening. On islands and ships all across the central Pacific, radio operators were listening . . . and hoping.

At 10:00 p.m., the NBC station in Honolulu made a special broadcast. "AMELIA EARHART . . . IF YOU CAN HEAR THIS SIGNAL, PLEASE RESPOND ON [FREQUENCY] 3105."

Within minutes, a station at Mokapu Point, on the Hawaiian island of Oahu, heard a faint signal on 3105, but it was "too weak to distinguish any words." At the same time, a Hawaiian coast guard station also heard a weak signal.

Twenty minutes later, *Itasca* also picked up signals. There was a voice, but the radiomen could not make out what it was saying. George Thompson immediately contacted the men on Howland Island. He wanted them to use their direction finder to get a bearing, which would tell them where the signal was coming from.

"Did you get a bearing?" Thompson asked one of the radiomen on Howland Island.

"No, will get one now," the radioman replied.

Thompson agreed to check back with him in half an hour.

It was now midnight, and NBC made another special broadcast. This time three military stations in Honolulu heard a reply. Unfortunately, the static was too thick to get a directional bearing. The coast guard's Hawaiian section also heard the signal. They could just make out a weak voice but could not understand what was being said. The U.S. Navy radio station at Wailupe (also on Oahu) also heard the voice, but again it was lost in static.

Aboard *Itasca*, it was time to contact Howland Island again. "Did you get a bearing?" Thompson asked.

"No," replied Howland's radioman, "the signals were very weak and when I shifted the direction-finding antenna the signal faded out completely."

Thompson suggested he check back in another hour, but the radioman on Howland Island had a different idea. "How about some sleep?" he asked.

Thompson agreed. Howland Island signed off. But signals continued to be heard.

This map shows the locations of various islands, radio stations and military bases across the Pacific. All were listening for messages from Amelia.

At 1:30 a.m. the radio station on Wake Island heard "a male voice although unreadable through static."

The coast guard station in California reported "a strong carrier being picked up by three receivers . . . signal is stronger from westerly direction."

And in the town of Wahiawa, about twenty miles from Honolulu, a Mr. Donaldson (his first name was lost in the official reports) heard a man's voice make "three or four calls." Donaldson was listening to programs on his Zenith radio when a man's voice broke through. He was able to make out the call letters KHAQQ, as well as the word "help." He immediately contacted the U.S. Navy radio station in Wailupe, which in turn forwarded the information to various search authorities.

At the exact time when Mr. Donaldson heard the man's voice, both Wake Island radiomen and the coast guard's Hawaiian section also heard a man's voice repeating Earhart's call letters, KHAQQ.

Minutes later, radiomen on Midway Island also heard the voice. Frustratingly, no one was able to take a bearing.

And then, suddenly, the airwaves fell silent. Aboard *Itasca*, the radiomen now heard only heavy static. The same went for the radio operators in Hawaii and California and on the islands of Wake, Midway and Mokapu. On Howland Island the radiomen were sound asleep.

But someone *was* claiming to hear a call from the missing plane—someone more than five thousand miles away.

Fame

1927 to 1928

WHILE AMELIA WAS WORKING AT Denison House—before she had received that mysterious call—the flying world was soaring forward.

In the spring of 1927, Charles Lindbergh did the seemingly impossible, flying nonstop across the North Atlantic. His thirty-three-hour flight from New York to Paris made aviation history and turned Lindbergh into a national hero. Everywhere he went, he was greeted with marching bands and ticker-tape parades. He received the Congressional Medal of Honor and was paid the unheard-of sum of $125,000 (almost one and a half million dollars nowadays) to write a book about his adventure. No one was more famous than Lindbergh.

Charles Lindbergh in the cockpit of the Spirit of St. Louis, *the plane he flew across the Atlantic.*

And other fliers longed to follow. Yes, Lindbergh had already accomplished a great challenge, but there were still others out there. There was the challenge of flying across the Atlantic to the United States against the wind—a harder, longer trip than Lindbergh's. There was the challenge of being the first to fly nonstop from New York to California, or nonstop from New York to Cuba. But the biggest remaining prize of all was to become the first woman to fly across the Atlantic.

In the year after Lindbergh's flight, five women attempted to fly across the Atlantic. Two of them each took along a male pilot because they did not have enough experience to fly alone as Lindbergh had. But this didn't matter to the public. The simple fact that a woman even dared to try caused great excitement.

Of the five women, two disappeared over the Atlantic, one had to be rescued at sea, and one never got her plane off the ground.

The fifth woman to try was the famous British aviatrix Elsie Mackay, who stunned fliers by taking off in March, when freezing temperatures still extended across the Atlantic. (In 1928, before the invention of deicers, ice was a plane's worst enemy.) Days later, parts of her plane washed up on Ireland's coast.

Who would try next?

Amy Phipps Guest decided she would. Wealthy, matronly, fifty-five-year-old Amy had never flown before. Still, she had a desire for adventure as well as a huge bank account. So, sparing no expense, she bought a plane from Commander Richard E. Byrd (who had used the plane on a flight around the North Pole) and sent it to an East Boston airfield so it could be fitted out for her flight. She told no one about her plans, not even her husband and children. The journey, she decided, would take place in May 1928. In her country estate in Roslyn, New York, she dreamed of making a dramatic landing, her plane touching down right in front of London's Houses of Parliament. Amy named the plane *Friendship*.

But somehow, Amy's family caught wind of her secret plans. They begged her not to do it. "You will end up floating in the ocean," wailed her daughter, Diana.

Amy backed down. But she still wanted an American to be the first woman to fly across the Atlantic. "Find me someone nice who will do us proud," she instructed her lawyer, David Layman. "I shall pay the bills." She went on to insist that the chosen woman should be "a lady, college-educated, attractive, and, if possible, a flyer."

"Is that all?" replied Layman sarcastically. He had no idea how to go about finding such a flier.

ENTER GEORGE PUTNAM

On the very day when David Layman was speaking with Amy Guest, the well-known publisher George Putnam was riding the Staten Island ferry. Putnam loved airplanes, and as luck would have it, he fell into conversation with a fellow passenger who just happened to be a pilot. The pilot passed on a fascinating piece of gossip: a wealthy woman had bought Commander Byrd's plane and was planning a long, dangerous and secret flight. The plane, added the pilot, was being outfitted in Boston.

"I instantly saw the possibilities," recalled George. "I had stumbled on an adventure-in-the-making which might provide a book."

George returned to his office to find that his old friend Hilton Railey had dropped by for a visit. Railey was a Boston public relations specialist who also had an interest in airplanes. George couldn't believe the coincidence. He repeated the gossip he'd heard on the ferry, then asked Railey to use his Boston connections to find out what he could.

Railey agreed. By midnight he had tracked down the plane and the name of the wealthy woman's lawyer: David Layman.

George Putnam telephoned Layman the very next morning. "I pretty much dropped from the clouds and introduced myself," said George. Layman, who was still struggling to find a female flier, eagerly accepted George's offer to help.

Now George turned again to Railey. Did Railey have any Boston contacts who might be able to help?

Railey did—a retired admiral named Reginald R. Belknap, who was very involved in the Boston air world.

Railey asked Belknap if he knew of a possible candidate.

"Why, yes," replied the admiral. "I know a young social worker who flies. . . . Call Denison House and ask for Amelia Earhart."

OPPORTUNITY COMES CALLING

A day later, Railey telephoned Amelia. "Would you be interested in doing something for aviation which might be dangerous?" he asked.

Intrigued, Amelia agreed to meet Railey at his office for an interview.

"How would you like to be the first woman to fly the Atlantic?" he asked her minutes after she'd walked in.

"Very much," replied Amelia.

Ten days later, she was invited to another interview with Railey in New York City. This time, George Putnam, as well as David Layman and Amy Guest's brother John Phipps, were there. (Having decided to leave all the details to her lawyer, Amy Guest wasn't present at the interview.) The men "rained questions upon me," remembered Amelia. "Was I willing to fly the Atlantic? What was my education? Was I strong? What flying experience did I have?"

The men were taken by her answers, as well as "her infectious laugh, her poise, warmth and impressive dignity." Additionally, they couldn't help noticing that Amelia looked enough like Charles Lindbergh to be his sister. "An added bonus, publicity-wise," remarked George.

Still, George was curious. "Why do you want to fly the Atlantic?" he asked her.

Amelia looked at him a moment, then smiled. "Why does a man ride a horse?" she replied.

This photograph of Amelia and George Putnam was taken in May 1928. He was, recalled one friend, "already mad about her."

"Because he wants to, I guess," answered George.

Amelia shrugged. "Well, then."

George laughed, and Amelia joined in.

Two days later she received a note from Mrs. Guest. "You may make this flight if you wish," wrote the older woman.

Recalled Amelia, "I couldn't say no."

PREPARATIONS

Amelia was made captain of the flight. This meant she would help make decisions, as well as keep the plane's log. But she would not take the plane's controls. This would be Bill Stultz's job. A skilled aviator, navigator and radio operator, Stultz had been hired as pilot months earlier. Lou "Slim" Gordon, a mechanic with years of engine experience, would also be on the flight.

Preparations for the trip were top-secret. "If it was known that a woman was trying to fly across the Atlantic, the airfield would be overrun with crowds," explained George.

Besides, they worried about competitors. "We didn't want to instigate a race," wrote Amelia. For this reason, she was asked to stay away from the airfield. "I did not dare show myself around the airport," she said. "Not once was I with the men on their test flights. In fact, I saw the *Friendship* only once before our first attempted take-off."

It was mid-May 1928 when she saw the plane for the first time—a Fokker with gold wings and an orange body (colors easy to spot if it went down in the sea). The Fokker had three 225-horsepower engines, two fuel tanks that could carry almost 900 gallons of gasoline, and pontoons in place of wheels so it could take off and land on water. Amelia thought the plane was beautiful. "Its golden wings," she wrote, "were strong and exquisitely fashioned."

While the plane was being readied, Amelia went on working at Denison House.

Even though she was sworn to secrecy, she didn't want to head off on such a dangerous journey without leaving some final word for her family. She decided to write farewell letters, "just in case."

To her father she wrote: "Hooray for the last grand adventure. I wish I had won, but it was worthwhile, anyway."

To her mother, she said: "My life has really been very happy, and I didn't mind contemplating its end in the midst of it."

And to Muriel, she wrote: "My only regret will be leaving you and Mother stranded."

While Amelia made preparations in case she died, George Putnam was making plans in case she lived. Arriving in Boston to personally take charge of the publicity, he sold Amelia's story rights to the *New York Times* and worked out a deal with Paramount Pictures for exclusive newsreel coverage of her takeoff and landing. More important, he hired Jake Coolidge, a renowned photographer, to take "a great bunch of shots" of her. George knew her photograph would be in demand if she succeeded.

In his spare time, George got to know Amelia better. He took her to restaurants and the theater. In return, she took him for rides in her sports car, which he dubbed the yellow peril because of her haphazard driving. He took to calling her A.E. She nicknamed him Simpkin, after the cat in Beatrix

The Friendship *in flight.*

"Lady Lindy"—one of the publicity shots taken by Jake Coolidge just before the transatlantic flight. Coolidge deliberately photographed Amelia in outfits similar to those worn by Lindbergh—leather jacket, white-edged helmet, riding breeches and goggles. He even used the same poses as those found in Lindbergh's most famous photographs. In the end, Amelia's resemblance to Lindbergh was uncanny.

Potter's story *The Tailor of Gloucester*. Together they discovered a mutual passion for speed, adventure and Chinese food.

"George was a fascinating man to Amelia," recalled Muriel. "He had been to the Arctic, was personal friends with some of the century's greatest explorers and adventurers, was handsome and intelligent."

Amelia fascinated George, too. He admired her poise, her dedication to hard work, her enthusiasm for airplanes. "He set about romancing her," recalled a friend, "with charm, wit and gifts."

One of those gifts was a leather-bound diary trimmed in gold and inscribed:

A.E.
From
G.P.
5/15/28

She would use this gift to record her thoughts and feelings during the flight.

Amelia obviously had romantic feelings for George, too. But she resisted his charms at first, because George was married. His wife, Dorothy Putnam, knew all about her husband's friendship with the pretty young pilot, and she fretted about it. "The minute he laid eyes on Amelia Earhart," Dorothy said later, "he had eyes for no one else."

IN FLIGHT

By late May, everything—the plane, the crew, the publicity—was in place. It was time to fly. But two attempts to take off from Boston failed because of bad weather. When the *Friendship* finally did take to the air (on June 3, 1928), it headed up the coast and into a thick fog. Since instruments for flying blind had not yet been invented, the crew looked for a hole in the fog and landed in Halifax, Nova Scotia.

The next day, with the skies clear again, they flew to Trepassey, Newfoundland. This was the jumping-off point for their trip across the Atlantic.

But days of strong gales and thick fog made takeoff impossible. The fliers spent the next week playing cards and growing more and more dispirited. Then George cabled with more bad news.

Their delay had opened up an opportunity for other female pilots. Hours earlier, Mabel Boll had announced her intention to start a transatlantic flight within the next few days. And in Germany, the aviatrix Thea Rasche also announced her plans to cross the Atlantic. Wrote Amelia in the plane's log, "our competitors are gaining on us."

She had to chance it. Bad weather or not, she decided, they would go.

The next day, June 12, the determined crew climbed into the *Friendship*. For the next four hours they battled to take off. But the "receding tide made the sea so heavy that the spray . . . drowned the outboard motors," wrote Amelia. "We are all too disappointed to talk."

The crew tried again the next morning, but still the weather made their efforts useless. "The days grow worse," Amelia wrote. "I think each time we have reached the low, but find we haven't."

To make matters worse, Bill was drinking heavily. Amelia lectured him about it, but he refused to listen. "There is a madness to Bill," she wrote, "which is not in keeping with a pilot who has to fly."

Finally, on June 17—after twelve days of waiting—the weather calmed a bit. "We are going today, and we are going to make it," Amelia declared. The problem was, Bill had been out drinking the night before and was in no shape to fly. Amelia spent hours pouring black coffee into her pilot in hopes of sobering him up. "She knew the start had to be made then or probably never," recalled Slim Gordon, "so finally, she simply got hold of her pilot and all but dragged him to the plane."

Slim cast off the mooring lines; then the plane taxied slowly across the choppy waves. But once again, it failed to take off. In the blustery winds, the aircraft was too heavy. So Amelia made a desperate decision. She ordered them to dump gasoline—all but 700 gallons. This meant that the fliers would have barely enough fuel to get across the Atlantic Ocean. Instead of landing in London as originally planned, they would now have to head for Ireland and hope they didn't get lost along the way. They simply didn't have enough gasoline to make any mistakes.

Finally—rocking and bouncing, its outboard motors sputtering from salt water spray—the *Friendship* staggered across the waves. In the plane's cabin Amelia crouched, stopwatch in hand. She was "checking the take-off time, and with my eyes glued on the air speed indicator as it slowly climbed. If it passed fifty miles an hour, chances were the *Friendship* could pull out and fly.

"Thirty—forty—the *Friendship* was trying again. A long pause, then the pointer went to fifty—fifty-five—sixty. We were off at last!"

They climbed to 3,000 feet and ran into fog. They climbed higher and met a snowstorm. Then Bill headed down, and they broke into clear skies and sunshine with a blue sea below them.

But not for long. The fliers soon found themselves in dense fog. "Not again on the flight did we see the ocean," wrote Amelia.

Unable to determine their course by sight, they hoped to rely on their radio. But somewhere over the Atlantic, the radio broke again. The *Friendship* could not get word from ships at sea to check their position. As the hours of flying continued, the tension aboard the plane increased. Their fuel was rapidly dwindling. If they were off course, they would be in serious trouble.

As captain of the flight, Amelia remained in the plane's bare cabin. It was so cold, she ended up wearing a fur-lined suit over her flying clothes.

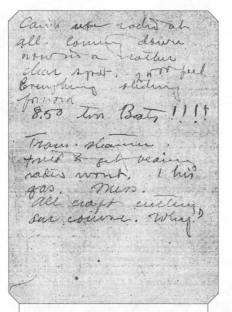

A page from Amelia's logbook shows her often scrawled handwriting. This entry reads:

Can't see land at all. Coming down now into a rather clear spot. 2400 feet Everything sliding forward 8.50 ton Boats!!!! Trans-steamer tried to get bearing radio wont. 1 hr gas. Mins. All craft cutting our course. Why?

With only one hour's fuel left, Bill dropped down through the clouds. Below them they saw a ship. Bill circled it, hoping its captain would paint the latitude and longitude on its deck (a common practice in those early aviation days). But the captain didn't. So Amelia wrote their request on a page torn from her logbook. She tied the note to an orange, then dropped it through the hatch in the cabin floor. It missed the ship and sank into the sea. So "we tried another shot," said Amelia. "No luck."

With their fuel now dangerously low, the fliers considered giving up and landing in the sea near the ship, where they would be picked up. Then Bill stubbornly declared, "That's out!" And he swung the plane back on course and kept straight on.

Minutes later, out of the mists grew a blue shadow. It was land.

Amelia cheered.

Slim yelled and tossed the sandwich he was eating out the window.

And Bill "permitted himself a smile" before bringing the *Friendship* down just as its motor sputtered out of gas. After a flight of twenty hours and forty minutes, they arrived at Burry Port (near Swansea), Wales, having passed just south of Ireland.

They tied up to a buoy near some railroad docks. "We were still some distance from shore," recalled Amelia. "The only people in sight were three men on the . . . beach. To them we waved, and Slim yelled lustily [for a boat]."

The men looked them over, then went back to work. "The *Friendship* simply wasn't interesting," said Amelia. Desperately, she waved a towel out the plane's front window.

"One friendly soul pulled off his coat and waved back," she remembered.

A whole hour passed before a boat finally came out, and three hours before the citizens of Burry Port realized that history had just landed in their little village. Word spread, and thousands of people turned out to greet the first woman to fly across the Atlantic. Amelia tried to tell them that the credit belonged to Bill and Slim. But the public only had eyes for her.

From the doorway of the Friendship, Amelia tries to get the attention of the people onshore.

CELEBRITY

Overnight, Amelia became a celebrity. The morning after the flight, President Calvin Coolidge sent her a congratulatory telegram; carmaker Henry Ford put a limousine at her disposal. In London (where she traveled the day after the landing), she met Winston Churchill—then chancellor of the British exchequer—and dined with members of royalty.

In late June she sailed for home, arriving in New York City on July 6 to a frenzied welcome. There were parades, receptions, medals awarded

From left to right, Bill Stultz, Amelia and Slim Gordon smile and wave during New York City's homecoming parade.

in New York, Boston and Chicago. There were interviews and photographs, magazine covers and product endorsements, newsreels and lectures and even a book deal. In August, George Putnam published Amelia's account of the flight, titled

20 Hrs., 40 min.: Our Flight in the Friendship. Consisting mainly of excerpts from her logbook, it was written during her three-week stay at the Putnams' Rye, New York, estate. Curiously, she dedicated it to Dorothy Putnam.

This cartoon, showing Amelia as "Lady Lindy" crossing the Atlantic with "Lady Luck," appeared in newspapers across the country on June 19, 1928.

Amelia typed away at her book, creating manuscript pages like this one.

How did Amelia feel about all the hoopla?

"She enjoyed the attention . . . the publicity," said Muriel. She was also "acutely aware of the fact that her fame would have been short-lived if not for George." In those days, fliers often made the front pages of the newspapers. But the public's interest never lasted long—usually only until the next aviator seized the headlines. George Putnam knew that once Amelia's name dropped out of the newspapers, she would be just another female pilot. So he exploited every opportunity to gain publicity for her. Through his vast connections, she met politicians and celebrities; she christened ships, cut ribbons, opened new buildings, gave speeches and interviews. And wherever she went, whatever she did, a newspaper photographer was always there to record the moment. George made sure of that.

Amelia saw the career George had mapped out for her—famous flier, lecturer, author— and she wanted it. Wrote one historian, "She was completely committed to the commercial property 'Amelia Earhart,' and was absolutely driven to make it a recognized name brand." She knew that if she wanted to fly, she would have to earn money. So she took all of George's

Between 1928 and 1937, Amelia was constantly in the limelight. This was essential, since flying was very expensive. In order to fly, she needed to raise money; in order to raise money, she needed to maintain her celebrity.

Amelia put it this way: "I make a record [flight] and then I lecture on it. That's where the money comes from. Until it's time to make another record."

George put it another way: "It is sheer, thumping hard work to be a hero."

And so Amelia endorsed products such as Kodak film, Stanavo engine oil, Franklin and Hudson automobiles and Lucky Strike cigarettes (even though she didn't smoke).

She had her photograph taken doing exciting things like parachuting, deep-sea diving and dining with movie stars.

This endorsement for cigarettes earned Amelia $1,500.

A deep-sea diving stunt in Long Island Sound resulted in a contract for a series of magazine articles.

She even went into business for herself, establishing the Amelia Earhart Clothing Company in 1933. Amelia herself designed the clothes, which sold exclusively in Amelia Earhart Shops in such upscale department stores as Macy's and Marshall Field's. "I have tried to put the

freedom that is in flying into my clothes," she said in an interview. "Good lines and good materials for women who lead active lives." Sadly, the fashion industry was too competitive, and Amelia's business lasted only a year.

An advertisement for clothing "designed by Amelia Earhart."

The best way to maintain celebrity and make money was by lecturing. Back in the days before television, the lecture circuit—even more so than radio and newsreels—was the most important way for popular figures to reach the public. Here was a chance for people in Terre Haute, Indiana, and Tacoma, Washington, to actually see and hear their heroes. For one night, at least, they could personally connect with the most famous and influential people of their time.

Amelia became a popular speaker on the lecture circuit. In 1933 alone, she delivered thirty-three talks in twenty-five days. In 1934 she appeared onstage 135 times, before audiences estimated at a total of eighty thousand. Between September 30

CONTINUED ON PAGE 60

CONTINUED FROM PAGE 59

and November 3, 1935, she crisscrossed her way from Youngstown, Ohio, to Michigan, on to Minnesota, through Nebraska, into Iowa, to Chicago, then down to central Illinois, into Indiana, back up to Michigan, back to Chicago, off to Missouri and Kansas, and back to Indiana, finally finishing in Wilmette, Illinois. "Life on the lecture tour is a real grind of one-night stands and one hotel after another," Amelia wrote to her mother. Still, she was earning between $250 and $300 for each lecture (about $3,500 nowadays), a tidy sum back then. Lecturing quickly became her major source of income. "The Earhart name had become a moneymaker," said one friend.

A flyer promoting one of Amelia's lectures.

advice to heart. "I was conscious of [his] brilliant mind and keen insight," she explained. "I recognized his tremendous power of accomplishments and respected his judgment."

As for George, he not only adored Amelia but also enjoyed her fame. It stroked his ego to know he had almost single-handedly made her one of the most famous women in the world. "It was fun," he said. He taught her how to talk into a microphone, avoid lowering her voice at the end of a sentence and smile with her lips closed so people wouldn't see the gap between her two front teeth.

When George—who was never far from her side—suggested she looked better without a hat, Amelia stopped wearing one. The hatless tousled curls became part of her image.

When George proposed she fly herself from speaking engagement to speaking engagement because "it was so much more thrilling to the public," Amelia did.

And when George advised her to make a donation to Commander Byrd's Antarctic expedition because it would add to her "charitable image," Amelia promptly wrote a check for $1,500. George made sure that news of her "selfless generosity" was published on the front page of the *New York Times*.

As one of their friends said, "It was [George] who provided the *design* for those adventures of hers, and pulled them off. I wonder if the slim, frail girl-in-slacks would have startled the world without the explosive, pragmatic apostle of the impossible to goad her on. . . . Both realized they had a good thing going and I suspect Amelia needed George more than he needed her."

After finishing her book, however, Amelia was also eager for something else. "All I wished to do in the world," she said, "was to be a vagabond—in the air."

Amelia's Little Plane

While in England after the transatlantic crossing, Amelia had test-flown a small sports plane known as the Avro Avian. She loved it. The Avian was fast and easy to handle, and so light that she could move it simply by picking up its tail and pulling. Its wings could even be folded up for easy storage. Anticipating some income from the success of the Atlantic flight, she bought the little plane and had it shipped to the United States. When it arrived in Boston weeks later, George laughed. "It's a bit of a pocket plane," he joked.

DANA'S STORY

Sixteen-year-old radio amateur Dana Randolph claimed he heard Amelia's cry for help.

"THIS IS AMELIA EARHART."

The voice that floated into the Rock Springs, Wyoming, living room sounded weak and whispery.

Sixteen-year-old Dana Randolph moved closer to his shortwave radio. Dana was fascinated with radios. For years he had studied and worked on them. He had even built his own sets. Just the day before, he had erected a brand-new antenna, one he had designed himself. He hoped the antenna would allow him to pick up radio stations from as far away as New York City, or maybe even London. But he had never expected this!

"This is Amelia Earhart," the voice said again. "Ship is on a reef south of the equator. Station KHAQQ." Then the signal died away.

Dana leaped to his feet. "Hey, Paw!" he hollered. "I got Miss Earhart!"

Dana's father ran into the room. Together they listened closely to the radio. At first they heard only static. Then the woman's voice came again from the speaker. She repeated her name and call letters, but as she gave her location, the signal disappeared.

"Everybody wants to know about that," said Dana's uncle, who had come into the room while father and son were listening. "Get downtown and report that."

Dana and his father hurried to the police station. The officer in charge directed them to the Department of Commerce Aeronautical Radio Facility that just happened to be right there in Rock Springs. After hearing Dana's story, the facility's radio operator notified navy officials in Washington, D.C. Then all three of them—Dana, his father and the radio operator—rushed back to the Randolphs' house. The flier's voice was still coming through the speakers. But the signal was so weak, no one could make out what she was saying.

Hours later, word of the incident reached *Itasca*. "Unconfirmed reports from Rock Springs, Wyoming state Earhart plane heard," read the message from the coast guard's San Francisco station. "Position on a reef southeast of Howland Island. This information may be authentic, as signals from mid-Pacific and Orient often heard inland when not audible on coast."

Could Dana's information be true? Was Amelia Earhart out there somewhere, calling for help?

Vagabonding Record Breaking and Romance

1928 to 1935

WITH HER BOOK WRITTEN, Amelia now turned to her next adventure, "vagabond[ing] in the air." She knew where she wanted to go—across the country to California. So she bought a handful of road maps, then headed west in the little Avian airplane she'd bought in England.

CROSS-COUNTRY FLIGHT

George went along with Amelia on the first leg of the trip. But he soon experienced the dangers of flying, when Amelia tried to land at Rodgers Field outside Pittsburgh. In those days, there were few airstrips, so pilots landed in any open space they could find. In this case, Amelia chose a farm field, complete with rocks, gullies and tree stumps. As the plane bumped across the uneven earth, it rolled into a ditch and flipped over.

"I was utterly petrified, but Amelia took it in stride," recalled George. She just pulled the plane out by its tail and assessed the damage—a broken propeller and cracked landing gear. In the 1928 world of flying, this sort of accident was common. Still, it was enough adventure for George. He returned to New York while Amelia had the plane repaired and continued with her flight.

Amelia did not have a planned route and simply landed whenever she felt hungry or tired. She became expert at coaxing food and lodging from complete strangers. Once she dropped down on an Illinois farm and was invited in for a chicken dinner. Another time she landed unexpectedly at an Oklahoma airstrip and was taken home by the field manager's wife for the night. "She said she hated to go to a hotel," the woman recalled. "What else could I do?"

In those early days of aviation, there were no navigational aids (other than magnetic compasses) to help pilots find their way. They flew simply by looking out their cockpit windows for landmarks or by using road maps. Amelia found her way by flying low and following roads, railroad tracks and rivers as they appeared on her map. But navigating in this manner was difficult. It was like "automobiling without signs," explained Amelia. "Imagine trying to recognize a new town the way flyers do—coming down through a hole in the clouds, you get a hundred-mile-an-hour look at a checkerboard of streets and roofs, trees and fields. . . . Do you manage to get a check on your location? Invariably not."

To make matters worse, the map lay open and pinned to her knee so it wouldn't blow out of the open cockpit. But one afternoon, over west Texas, a strong wind snatched the map away. Needing gasoline, she followed cars on the road below and, just before darkness, spied the tiny town of Hobbs, New Mexico. After bringing the plane down, Amelia broke every traffic law in town as she rolled along East Broadway to the filling station at Thomson's Grocery. The good-natured townspeople helped her fold up the plane's wings and move it to a safe place for the night. They fed her a supper of meat loaf and mashed potatoes at the Owl Café, gassed up her plane and gave her a bed for the night. The next morning after breakfast (but still without a map), she once again set off for California.

Amelia arrived at Mines Field in Los Angeles on September 14, 1928. Two weeks later, she turned around and headed back to the East Coast. When she arrived, she discovered that, without knowing it, she had become the first woman to fly from the Atlantic to the Pacific and back again.

While she'd been away, George had lined up several public appearances for her. Amelia welcomed these opportunities. "There is so much to be gained from them," she told her mother. There certainly was. In return for saying a few words during NBC radio's broadcast of the National Car Show, she was given a blue Chrysler roadster. And after she endorsed an expensive fur-lined flying suit, one Fifth Avenue department store made her one. Joked Amelia, "Is there anything I can say about Tiffany's?"

Around this time, George also finagled an invitation for her to join the staff of *Cosmopolitan* magazine as its first aviation editor. Nearly every month for the next year she wrote articles with titles such as "Try Flying Yourself" and "Is It Safe to Fly?" But talking and writing about flying weren't as fulfilling as the real thing.

Amelia published her first article as Cosmopolitan's aviation *editor in the November 1928 issue.*

RACE!

In 1929, Amelia learned that the first airplane race for women, called the Women's Air Derby, would be held in August. It was an exciting prospect for female fliers (until now, only men had raced airplanes). Starting out from Santa Monica, California, and ending in Cleveland, Ohio, it would be a true test of women's navigational and piloting skills. It was, claimed Amelia, "a chance to play the game as men play it, by rules established for them as flyers, not as women."

She was eager to enter the race. But if she was going to make a good showing, she knew she needed to fly something bigger and more powerful than her Avian.

Her first choice was the big six-passenger Bellanca. But the plane maker—who chose his customers carefully to protect the reputation of his product—refused to sell her one. He didn't think she was skilled enough to fly such a large plane. So Amelia turned to the Lockheed Vega. Looking much like a speeding bullet, the Vega was sleek, streamlined and fast. "A sure winner," said George.

But did Amelia have the skills to handle such a powerful plane? George was concerned. Not long after she bought the Vega, he telephoned teenage aviatrix Elinor Smith. Just sixteen years old, Smith had become the youngest licensed pilot in the world. Already she had set an alti-

Amelia peeks happily from the cockpit window of her Lockheed Vega, 1928.

tude record and made headlines when she flew, illegally, under all four bridges on New York City's East River. Coincidentally, she was now working as a demonstration pilot for Bellanca aircraft—the same company Amelia had tried to purchase a plane from just weeks earlier.

What did George want from Elinor Smith?

Her experience in flying big planes, of course. He offered Elinor seventy-five dollars a week (an enormous sum in 1929) to pilot Amelia in the derby, as well as around the country during an upcoming nationwide lecture tour. "But of course," continued George, "she must appear to be doing it. When pictures are taken at various stops, you must stand to her left, so her name will always come up first in the captions."

The teenager declined his offer and wondered how "Miss Earhart would [eventually] cope with the unwieldy plane." Later she heard rumors that Amelia was

Not Very Nice

George and Amelia could be ruthless in their quest to make her the leading female pilot. Once, when Lady Mary Heath (England's foremost aviatrix and a friend of Amelia's) arrived in the United States for a lecture tour she had booked months earlier, she discovered that all her events had been canceled. Who had been slotted in Lady Heath's place? Amelia Earhart! George had convinced the lecture-tour company that Amelia was "of greater interest to audiences."

"At this point," said Lady Heath, "my friendship for Amelia quickly waned."

taking secret flying lessons at a private airstrip near George's home in Rye, New York. "I hoped so, for her sake," said Elinor.

When the derby's starting flag went down months later—on August 18—nearly every noteworthy American woman pilot was at the starting line. (Elinor Smith had hoped to enter but instead took a job giving flying demonstrations to the crowds awaiting the racers in Cleveland.) Amelia and eighteen other contestants soared off into the clouds. Problems quickly arose. On the second day of the race, Marvel Crosson's airplane dove to the ground, killing her instantly. Minutes later, Claire Fahy was forced down after her wing braces snapped.

Amelia led on the second day, but on a refueling stop in Arizona, she overshot the runway and upended the Vega when it hit a sandbank. Her propeller was bent, but a new one was quickly flown in from California. Within hours she was back in the sky.

Other pilots were having problems, too. Blanche Noyes was flying over Texas when she looked over her shoulder and saw that her plane was on fire. Landing, she quickly threw sand on the flames, then took off again despite damage to her plane's undercarriage. And one flier, Margaret Perry, got sick. She had begun the race with what she thought was a case of the flu. Two days later she wound up in the hospital with typhoid fever.

On the seventh day of the race, the fliers arrived in Columbus, Ohio. Ruth Nichols was in the lead, followed by Louise Thaden and then Amelia. Each pilot tried to make the best time on this last leg of the race to Cleveland. Ruth took off before the others. But as she taxied down the runway, one wing dipped and she lost control. The plane hit a tractor and flipped over. Ruth was unhurt, but her plane was destroyed. She was out of the race.

The next day, Louise Thaden victoriously crossed the finish line in Cleveland, with Gladys O'Donnell a close second. Amelia limped in a disappointing third. Even though she had the fastest plane, her flying time was two whole hours slower than Thaden's.

Elinor Smith remembered Amelia's poor landing in Cleveland. The Vega bounced across the length of the airport, with Amelia desperately trying to brake and avoid a ground loop (a circular skid). "I was filled with admiration for her," said Elinor. "It was barely five months since the [plane's purchase] . . . and there was absolutely no way she could have built up enough air time to be at ease behind the controls of the fastest heavy monoplane in the air. . . . One look at her drawn countenance when she flipped up the cockpit hood" told Elinor and the other pilots who had watched the performance that "this was gut courage that transcended the sanity of reasoning."

Amelia and her fellow contestants in the 1929 Women's Air Derby, with the Vega in the background. Note the trophies.

WHAT NEXT?

After the derby, Amelia turned her attention to other aeronautical feats. In her Vega she set the women's speed record by flying 181 miles per hour. She set a new altitude record by climbing to 18,415 feet. And she helped to establish the first organization of women pilots in the world. Called the Ninety-Nines because it started with ninety-nine licensed women pilots, it provided support for its members and advanced the science of aviation. Amelia was elected as its first president.

She also spent lots of time with George. Recalled Amelia, "We both loved the outdoors, books, and sport. And so we lunched together, and dined together, took horseback rides together . . ."

People who saw them had no doubt about their relationship. "Their love affair was in full swing," said one friend. "There was an electricity between them that you couldn't miss, and the subtle pats and touching were unmistakable."

Dorothy Putnam realized what was happening, too. Just weeks after the Women's Air Derby—during a celebrity-studded barbecue at their Rye home—Dorothy decided to move out. One guest remembered what happened next:

> I wandered around to the front of the house. An express truck was parked outside, and I opened the door to see two movers carrying a trunk from the second floor. Dorothy Putnam . . . followed them downstairs, dressed in her traveling clothes.
>
> "Didn't you know? I'm divorcing George," she said. "He doesn't need me anymore."
>
> I strolled back to the party where [George] was gaily spearing frankfurters for Amelia Earhart.

Once his divorce was final, George begged Amelia to marry him. Amelia cherished her freedom and had always been deeply suspicious of marriage. "It's a bit like a cage, isn't it?" she'd once asked her mother. When a friend asked her straight out if she would ever consider marrying George, Amelia cried, "No!"

But George persisted. For almost two years he proposed over and over again. "I was turned down six times at least," he later admitted. Finally, in November 1930, Amelia said yes. "He wore me down," she explained to reporters.

Amelia wasn't completely comfortable with the idea of marriage, though. She still worried about losing her independence and individuality. So on the day of their wedding—February 7, 1931—she handed George a letter. In it she wrote:

"I must exact a cruel promise, and that is you will let me go in a year if we find no happiness together."

George agreed, and the two were married at his mother's house in upstate New York. It was a no-fuss affair. The bride wore a plain brown suit and sensible shoes. About the event, the *New York Times* wrote:

> The ceremony itself . . . [took] but five minutes. The only witnesses were Mr. Putnam's mother; his uncle . . . and twin black cats. As Mr. Putnam slipped a plain platinum ring on Miss Earhart's finger the cats, coal black and playful, rubbed arched backs against his ankles.

Between lecturing, writing and flying, the newlyweds spent time at their Rye estate. For the first time, Amelia had her own home, and she enjoyed it. She rearranged furniture and even bought herself two canaries, something she had wanted "for ever so long." She also started work on a second book, writing about her childhood and her early flying adventures. The book, titled *The Fun of It: Random Records of My Own Flying and of Women in Aviation*, was published in 1931.

But during all this time, a new idea was forming. One morning over breakfast, she asked George, "Would you *mind* if I flew the Atlantic?"

It was the first time anyone had heard her mention such a trip. But Amelia must have been thinking

Was It Love?

Why did Amelia finally marry George?

An interview she gave a few years after their wedding provides a few clues. She said:

I had no special feelings about Mr. Putnam at first. I was too absorbed in the prospects of the trip and of my being the one to make it. . . . Of course after I had talked to him for very long I was conscious of the brilliant mind and keen insight of the man. . . . We came to depend on each other, yet it was only friendship between us, or so—at least—I thought at first. At least I didn't admit even to myself that I was in love . . . but at last the time came, I don't quite know when it happened, when I could deceive myself no longer. I couldn't continue telling myself that what I felt for GP was only friendship. I knew I had found the one person who could put up with me.

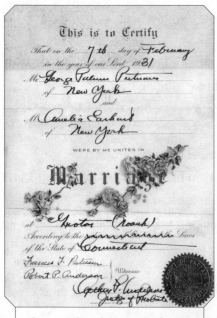

George and Amelia's marriage license, dated February 7, 1931.

George and Amelia Putnam at home in Rye, New York.

about it since her first flight across the Atlantic in 1928. For her, that adventure had been "incomplete," because she hadn't flown it solo. "I received more credit than I felt I deserved," she later said. "Now I wanted to justify myself to myself. I wanted to prove that I deserved at least a small fraction of the nice things said about me."

There was another reason, too. Several other female pilots were preparing to make the flight. If one of them crossed the Atlantic first, it could ruin Amelia's career. She had to beat them.

George understood all this and was enthusiastic about the idea. With his keen sense of story, he proposed a date for the flight—May 20, 1932, the fifth anniversary of Charles Lindbergh's famous solo flight.

Amelia liked the idea, but the proposed date was only five months away. Was it possible to get ready in so short a time?

They both believed so, and George flung himself into preparations. He hired aeronautical experts, who added extra fuel tanks to both wings and the cabin of the Vega. They strengthened the fuselage with braces so it could support the increased weight of the added fuel. And they put in a 500-horsepower supercharged engine, as well as the latest in navigational instruments. (These were still very basic. Amelia's plane was fitted with an altimeter, which displayed altitude, and an altitude gyroscope, which would tell her the plane's orientation when she could not see.)

Amelia prepared for the trip, too. She practiced flying with a hood, a big visor that allowed her to see only the instruments. In this way she learned to handle the plane using the instruments alone, without looking outside. This time if fog closed in, she wouldn't lose her course.

Like those for her first trip across the Atlantic, these preparations were made in secret. No one, not even her mother, was told. "A.E.'s life must remain as normal as possible," directed George. Secrecy ensured that there were no reporters hanging around pushing for interviews; no photographers tripping over airplane parts; no bags of fan mail begging to be answered. Right now he wanted Amelia to focus all her energy on the upcoming trip. There would be plenty of time for publicity afterward.

ALONE IN THE NIGHT SKY

On May 20, 1932, Amelia took off from Harbour Grace, Newfoundland, the official starting point of the journey. (She had flown from New York the day before, leaving George behind.) In her cockpit she had some canned tomato juice and a few squares of chocolate, and around her wrist she wore her lucky elephant-toe bracelet, the one George had given her weeks earlier. A photographer snapped a few last pictures, and when he begged for "just one more," she obliged and smiled. Then she settled into the cockpit, waved goodbye

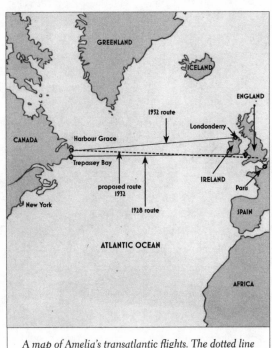

A map of Amelia's transatlantic flights. The dotted line indicates the route she had planned to take to Paris.

to the small crowd that had gathered, and roared off down the field. It was 7:12 p.m.

The Vega climbed into the moonlit sky. It was such a clear evening that she could see icebergs and fishing boats on the water below. But as darkness fell, the altimeter failed. Now she had no way of knowing how far above the ocean she was flying. Still, the stars and the moon were bright. Visibility was good. Amelia calmed herself. She could manage without the instrument. That was when she smelled burning oil.

Looking out, she saw a small blue flame licking through a broken weld where hot exhaust gases escaped from the plane's cylinders. It was worrisome, but she pressed on. The flame, she decided, was confined to the broken weld. She didn't think the fire would spread.

Soon the moon disappeared behind thick, black clouds, and she found herself in a rainstorm that quickly turned to an ice storm. Ice coated the windshield, the wings and then the mechanisms. The Vega went into a spin. "How long we spun, I do not know," she later wrote. She did what she had to do—she descended so the warmth of the lower altitude would melt the ice. Often she dipped "too close for comfort" to the ocean's whitecaps, flying just above breaking waves. As dawn broke, the storm lifted. With a sigh of relief, Amelia climbed once more, breaking into "brilliant sunlight on top of white clouds that looked like endless snowfields."

But now the broken weld was shaking badly, and when she turned on her reserve fuel tank, she discovered that its gauge was leaking. Gasoline trickled down her neck. It was the last straw. Although she had planned on landing in Paris as Lindbergh had five years earlier, she now decided to land at the first possible place.

Coming down, she saw a meadow. Circling it twice, she chose her spot, then landed beside a herd of grazing cows as an astonished farmer watched.

Amelia cut the switches and climbed out of her plane. "Where am I?" she called to the farmer.

Amelia poses for photographers the day after her solo transatlantic flight.

President Herbert Hoover sent this congratulatory telegram to Amelia: I VOICE THE PRIDE OF THE NATION IN CONGRATULATING YOU . . . YOU HAVE DEMONSTRATED NOT ONLY YOUR OWN DAUNTLESS COURAGE BUT ALSO THE CAPACITY OF WOMEN TO MATCH THE SKILL OF MEN IN CARRYING THROUGH THE MOST DIFFICULT FEATS OF HIGH ADVENTURE.

On November 20, 1932, Amelia was speaking in Poughkeepsie, New York, about her solo flight across the Atlantic when a tall woman entered the room. The audience buzzed. It was Eleanor Roosevelt, wife of president-elect Franklin D. Roosevelt. "I hope to know Miss Earhart more and more but I never hope to admire her more than I do now," said Mrs. Roosevelt, who had driven the thirty minutes from her home to meet the flier. "She has done so many things which I have always wanted to do."

It was the beginning of their friendship. Eleanor longed to pilot her own plane. Amelia immediately offered to teach her, and arranged for the eye tests required for a student pilot's permit. Six weeks later—having passed the tests—Eleanor sent the permit to Amelia with a note that said, "The question now comes as to whether or not I can induce my husband to let me take lessons." Franklin, however, said no, and Eleanor gave up her dream. But she continued to love flying.

And she continued to admire Amelia. On April 20, 1933, just weeks after Franklin's presidential inauguration, Eleanor invited the Putnams to dinner at the White House. Afterward, Amelia asked her friend if she wanted to experience night flying for the first time. Eleanor did. So, dressed in their elegant silk gowns and white gloves (and accompanied by several reporters), they headed over to the Washington, D.C., airstrip and boarded a small passenger airplane owned by Eastern Airlines. Amelia had the cabin lights turned out so Eleanor could experience the full wonder of the twinkling lights below. She also spent a little time demonstrating that she could fly the plane. Eleanor even took her turn in the cockpit so the captain could explain the controls to her.

That evening cemented their friendship. From then on, whenever Amelia was in Washington, she stayed at the White House. She supported Franklin when he ran for president again in 1936, and made public appearances with Eleanor on his behalf.

As for Eleanor, she thought so much of Amelia that she kept a copy of the flier's poem "Courage Is the Price" in the desk drawer where she stored special items that gave her strength and inspiration. It read:

Courage is the price that
Life exacts from granting peace.

The soul that knows it now
Knows no release from little things:
Knows not the livid loneliness of fear,
Nor the mountain heights where bitter joy can
   hear the sound of wings.
Nor can life grant us boon of living,
   compensate
For dull gray ugliness and pregnant hate
Unless we dare
The soul's dominion.
Each time we make a choice, we pay
With courage to behold the restless day,
And count it fair.

From an airplane window, Amelia points out the White House to Eleanor Roosevelt on their night flight.

"In Gallagher's pasture," he replied. The pasture was in Londonderry, Northern Ireland.

In spite of everything that had gone wrong, she had achieved her goal. She had become the first woman to fly solo two thousand miles across the Atlantic.

MORE CHALLENGES

But Amelia didn't rest on her laurels. Just three months later she set a new all-time speed record by flying the 2,400 miles from New York to Los Angeles in nineteen hours, five minutes. Eleven months after that, she flew the same course and set another record: seventeen hours, seven minutes.

On January 11, 1935, she tackled a new challenge: flying across 2,400 miles of Pacific Ocean from Hawaii to California. Other pilots had flown from California to Hawaii, but no one had made a successful west-to-east trip. She took off from Honolulu. "Contrasted to the Atlantic crossings, this was a journey of stars, not storms; of tropic loveliness instead of ice," she later wrote.

It was an uneventful trip. Amelia flew through a "touch of rain" and some "wearying fog," and after seventeen hours, California's coastal hills

A Radio First

For the Hawaii-to-California flight, George insisted that a two-way radio be installed in his wife's plane—the first time Amelia had ever had one on board. The equipment allowed her to pick up radio stations as well as communicate directly with them. George also insisted that Amelia make regular contact at a quarter to and a quarter past each hour. This she did, in an unprofessional way. "Everything is okay," she would report.

The sound of her voice was a comfort to George, who was listening for her at the KGU commercial radio station in Honolulu. "This feature was a pleasant contrast to previous Atlantic flights with their long blank silences," said George.

Amelia thought the radio was a revelation, too. While she listened, in flight, to the KGU radio station, the music suddenly stopped and the announcer's voice said, "We are interrupting our musical program with an important news flash. Amelia Earhart has just taken off from Honolulu on an attempted flight to Oakland, California."

Inside her cockpit, Amelia smiled. "You're telling me!" she thought.

The announcer continued, "Mr. Putnam will try to communicate with his wife."

Then George's voice filled the plane. Recalled Amelia, "It was thrilling to have his voice come in so clear to me, sitting out there over the Pacific."

When the plane's mechanic later asked what she thought of the two-way radio, she grinned. "Miraculous!" she exclaimed.

The welcome at Oakland airfield after Amelia completed the first solo flight from Hawaii to the United States, in 1935. Thousands turned out to cheer Amelia's landing, a testament to George's publicity skills.

Every Sunday in the late 1930s, newspapers ran this cartoon series depicting the feats of legendary pilots. Amelia's feature ran on March 24, 1935. She was one of just two women highlighted during the strip's ten-year run.

came into view. Minutes later she flew over San Francisco Bay and touched down in Oakland. She was now the biggest star in aviation's history—the first person (male or female) to make a solo flight from Hawaii to California, the first to fly solo over a sizable portion of the Pacific and the first to solo over both the Atlantic and the Pacific.

But it still wasn't enough. Amelia felt compelled to fly, and George went along with her wishes. Three months later she took off on another record-breaking flight—this time becoming the first person to fly solo from Los Angeles to Mexico City, a thousand-mile trip. It was an easy journey—soaring over mountains and desert—until a bug flew into her eye. Unable to read her map, she landed in a cactus-dotted field and asked directions.

"Cowboys and villagers sprang up miraculously," wrote Amelia. And even though her Spanish "did not exist, and none of the vaqueros spoke English," they managed to point her in the right direction. Half an hour later she landed in Mexico City.

She didn't stay long. Eight days later she pointed the Vega toward New York City, 2,185 miles north. The route took her over 700 miles of the Gulf of Mexico. It was a clear day with few clouds, and she could see everything that lay below. This was a first for Amelia. Her other ocean crossings had been made mostly at night, usually in heavy fog or clouds. But much of this crossing was made in daylight. "My imagination toyed with the idea of what would happen if the single engine of my Lockheed Vega should conk," she wrote.

At that moment she resolved to never again fly her Vega over water. "I promised myself that any further over-ocean flying would be attempted in a plane with more than one motor, capable of keeping aloft with a single engine. Just in case."

She already knew which plane she wanted—a Lockheed Electra. The Electra was unlike any other plane being manufactured at the time. It could carry twelve people, had a wingspan of 55 feet, was almost 39 feet long, could soar to an altitude of 19,000 feet, and could fly 2,000 miles without refueling.

What would she do with such a huge twin-engine plane?

"There was one flight which I most wanted to attempt—to fly around the globe at its waistline, the equator."

It was, Amelia recalled, "the beginning of the world flight project."

Paid Stunt or Heroic Adventure?

Up until 1935, Amelia's career had been almost entirely free of criticism. Occasionally, cartoons or newspaper editorials took jabs at her, claiming that women had no place in aviation. But no one ever questioned her reason for flying. "We believe Miss Earhart's passion for flying is perhaps matched only by her desire to demonstrate that women are equals of men in the air or out of it," wrote one magazine.

All that changed when the public learned that Amelia had been paid $10,000 by the Hawaiian Sugar Planters' Association to make the Hawaii-to-California flight in hopes of generating publicity for the islands. And the planters definitely got their money's worth. Not only was the public's eye trained on Hawaii during the trip, but afterward Amelia plugged the islands in interviews and on the lecture circuit. "I have no idea how many people bought pineapple as a result of AE's flight . . . or how many people got a first urge to see Hawaii," bragged George.

Some people started believing that the flight was just a paid stunt. "The fact that she was privately paid this amount to promote Hawaiian interests strikes us as unseemly," complained the weekly journal the *Nation*. Even her old friend Hilton Railey said sourly, "Amelia has gotten caught up in the hero racket."

Amelia felt that the criticism was unfair. "The greatest hazard I had to overcome [on this flight] was the criticism heaped on my head for even contemplating the flight." She claimed she would have made the flight "with or without [the planters'] support."

BETTY'S STORY

THOUSANDS OF MILES FROM THE CENTRAL PACIFIC, fifteen-year-old Betty Klenck settled down in front of her family's top-of-the-line radio set to listen to some afternoon programs. Her father, a radio buff, had even rigged up a special antenna that stretched across the backyard from the house to a nearby utility pole. The results were incredible. Even though the Klenck family lived in St. Petersburg, Florida, they picked up signals from as far way as Mexico and sometimes even Europe. Betty loved nothing better than turning the shortwave dial in search of these "exotic programs." While she listened, she liked to doodle in a notebook she kept beside the radio.

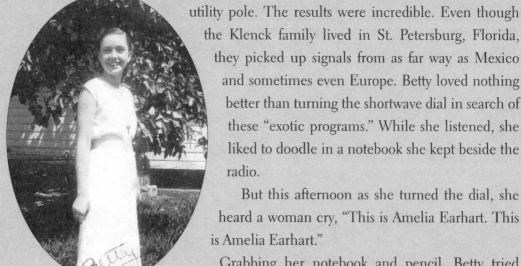

Betty Klenck in the backyard of her St. Petersburg home.

But this afternoon as she turned the dial, she heard a woman cry, "This is Amelia Earhart. This is Amelia Earhart."

Grabbing her notebook and pencil, Betty tried to write down everything she heard. Sometimes the words came too fast. Other times static made it hard to hear. And every once in a while the signal faded out, disappearing for a few minutes before finally returning.

"Help me," Betty claims the woman said, and then, "Water's high." She was interrupted by a ruckus in the background.

According to the teenager, a man then cried, "Help, help, I need air."

To Betty it sounded as if the man and woman were in a small space, like a plane. And as she kept listening, she became convinced that the plane had crashed on land but was slowly filling with water.

Two pages from the notebook Betty kept beside her family's radio. The first page shows the doodling she often did while listening. The second shows some of the notes taken the day she heard a woman calling for help. While most of the entries are self-explanatory—"send us help," "let me out of here," "take it away Howland"—a few are more difficult to interpret. What might "N.Y. N.Y. N.Y." mean? And who is Marie? We can only speculate.

Over the years, Betty tried to share her notebook with government officials, but no one paid it any attention. They dismissed it as the mere scribbling of a fifteen-year-old girl. She had given up thinking anyone would ever believe her when a friend happened to see the TIGHAR Web site. TIGHAR (The International Group for Historic Aircraft Recovery) is one of the leading aviation archaeological foundations in the country. Betty's friend sent a message to the group. Intrigued, members of the group examined the notebook. And while experts have not yet authenticated it beyond all doubt, it does appear to be a real-time transcription. As for Betty, she spent the rest of her life feeling "a deep sadness that I couldn't do anything for [Amelia]."

"Where are you going?" Betty recorded the woman as saying. "We can't bail out. See?"

"Yes," said the man.

"Yes," said the woman.

Then the man cried, "Oh, oh, ouch!"

The woman asked, "Are you so scared . . . What?"

It went on like this for almost two hours, with Betty listening and writing. Toward the end of the signal, Betty got the impression that the water was moving the plane. The woman seemed to bang her arm on something accidentally, and she let out a long string of curse words. Then the voices faded away.

"I was home alone," Betty recalled. "But as soon as Dad got home from work and heard the last part of her cries for help, he immediately drove to the coast guard station."

The coast guard, however, refused to listen to Mr. Klenck. "They wouldn't do anything for [Amelia]," said Betty, because they didn't believe someone in Florida could pick up signals from the Electra's transmitter. "I guess they didn't know about our specially built antenna," she added.

Had the teenager really heard the lost flier?

If so, Betty Klenck may have been the last person in the world to hear Amelia Earhart's voice.

Plans

1935 to 1937

WHILE AMELIA DREAMED OF AN AROUND-THE-WORLD FLIGHT IN A BIGGER PLANE, an unusual opportunity presented itself.

"We want you at Purdue University," the school's president, Edward C. Elliott, told her in the spring of 1935.

"What would I do?" asked Amelia. Without any teaching qualifications, she wondered how she could contribute.

But Elliott knew. He wanted the flier to inspire Purdue's female students to take up careers in such male-dominated fields as agriculture and engineering.

The idea appealed to Amelia. Women, she believed, should be encouraged to take chances. They should look beyond the comfort and security of marriage and instead "dare to live." She once told an audience, "There are a great many boys who would be better off making pies, and a great many girls who would be better off as mechanics." Now she eagerly agreed to spend part of the 1935–1936 school year on Purdue's campus.

Amelia chose to live in the women's residence hall, where she delighted her dorm mates with her independent behavior. She put her elbows on the table during meals and once showed up for dinner in flying clothes rather than the required

EveryWeek *magazine ran this article on Amelia's new job at Purdue.*

skirt. This behavior caused ripples. When the students tried following Amelia's example, the housemother scolded, "As soon as you fly the Atlantic, you may!"

But Amelia's influence with the female students went far deeper than table manners. After dinner the girls often followed her into the housemother's den, where they nibbled cookies and talked late into the night. Sitting cross-legged on the floor, Amelia led the discussions. "[They] centered around Miss Earhart's belief that women . . . really did have choices about what we could do with our lives," recalled one student. "'Study whatever you want,' she counseled us girls. 'Don't let the world push you around.'"

Amelia was such a popular teacher that the school's enrollment of female students increased by fifty percent. Everyone, it seemed, wanted to take one of her classes.

That same fall, Amelia told a reporter that she couldn't break any more flying records because her Vega was too old. "I'm looking for a tree on which new and better airplanes grow, and I'm looking for a shiny new one to shake down."

George knew just the tree to shake—Purdue University. Sitting down with President Elliott, he suggested the idea of a "Flying Laboratory," in which Amelia could study the effects of air travel. It would be, persisted George, "an aeronautical first."

This idea bubbled in President Elliott's mind until a dinner party at his home a few weeks later. There Amelia talked about her dreams for women and aviation, and how she would like her next flight to be "a thorough check of modern

Science or a Racket?

Amelia's announcement of her "Flying Laboratory" and her proposed around-the-world flight was met with sharp criticism. In his widely circulated newspaper column, aviation writer Alford Williams—a highly respected flier and a leader in aircraft development—scoffed at the aviator and her motives. He wrote:

> Like every other human enterprise, aviation suffers from a great number of ingeniously contrived rackets. Daring courageous individuals with nothing to lose and all to gain have used and are using aviation merely as a means toward quick fortune and fame. The worst racket of all is that of individually sponsored trans-oceanic flying . . . [where] the personal profit angle in dollars and cents, and the struggle for personal fame, have been camouflaged and presented under a banner of "scientific progress."

> . . . Amelia Earhart's "Flying Laboratory" is the latest and most distressing racket that has been given to a trusting and enthusiastic public. There's nothing in that "Flying Laboratory" beyond duplicates of the controls and apparatus found on board every major airline transport, and no one ever sat at the controls of her "Flying Laboratory" who knew about the technical side of aviation. . . . Nothing is said about the thousands of dollars she and her manager-husband expect to [earn]. Nothing at all was hinted of the fat lecture contracts, the magazine and book rights for stories of the flight. . . . No, the whole affair was labeled "purely scientific" for public consumption. . . . It's high time that the Bureau of Air Commerce puts an end to aviation's biggest racket—"Purely Scientific" ballyhoo.

equipment. I expect to keep a log of what happened to personnel and machine under various conditions. Records such as these . . . can do much to safeguard subsequent flights," she said.

One of the other dinner guests, David Ross, was so impressed by Amelia's words that he offered to donate $50,000 toward buying her a plane. Over the next few months, further donations totaling an additional $30,000 in money and equipment came from J. K. Lilly (of the Eli Lilly drug company), Vincent Bendix (a car and airplane inventor and an industrialist) and the manufacturing companies Western Electric, Goodrich and Goodyear.

The next spring, Elliott announced the creation of the Amelia Earhart Fund for Aeronautical Research for the purpose of "develop[ing] scientific and engineering data of vital importance to the aviation industry." The fund's first purchase would be an $80,000 (one million dollars nowadays) twin-engine customized Lockheed

Electra, so that Amelia Earhart could pursue the long-distance flights she dreamed of. The plane's title would be in her name, and decisions about how the plane would be used would be hers alone.

Amelia took possession of her new plane on her thirty-ninth birthday, July 24, 1936. The Electra was breathtaking. "I could write poetry about that ship," she gushed after she flew it for the first time.

A NEW ADVENTURE

Now Amelia began giving serious thought to her new adventure—circling the globe at the earth's middle. That was the longest way to do it—27,000 miles. More important, it was the most *novel* way to do it.

Amelia knew that the winds of aviation were changing. The public was tiring of record-breaking flights. Almost every major record had been broken, and all the major flight routes (across oceans and countries) had been spanned. In fact, by 1936 commercial airlines had made it possible for *anyone* to fly as a passenger across the Pacific.

What was so special about long-distance stunt flying now? Not much. According to historian Susan Ware, "The only thing left was to find new routes or to do old ones faster or with a twist or gimmick."

Flying around the world, however, was hardly unique. Between 1924 and 1933, six different expeditions had circled the globe, including one solo flight made by the famous pilot Wiley Post. Amelia's only novelty was taking the long equatorial route around the world. That and being a woman. (It should be noted that although Amelia initially planned to circle the globe all by herself, she soon saw problems with this plan and decided to take along a navigator who could help find the way across long stretches of jungle and ocean.)

When George asked why she wanted to attempt such a trip, she replied, "It is my frosting on the cake."

"Life is full of other challenges," he insisted.

Pilots like Amelia Earhart and Charles Lindbergh weren't the only ones taking to the air in the 1920s and 1930s. Regular Americans were, too. But they weren't handling the controls themselves. They were flying as passengers.

It was the United States Post Office that gave passenger airlines the boost they needed. The post office began using airplanes to deliver the mail in 1920. By 1925, these planes were delivering 14 million packages and letters a year. And in that time, the post office had maintained regular flight schedules, created airports across the country, and established air routes. That was when the government decided to transfer airmail service to private companies. The government believed that private companies could transport the mail more efficiently. In return, private companies would pay the government for use of those established air routes.

Private companies eagerly bid for the air routes. And the winners became transportation giants. There was Pan American Airways, which was awarded the New York-to-Boston route; American Airlines, which received the St. Louis-to-Chicago route; and Transcontinental and Western Air (TWA), which won the Salt Lake City-to-Los Angeles route. These companies now began pouring money into passenger travel technology, and by 1928, Boeing had introduced a plane that could carry seventeen passengers.

But air travel at this time was primitive. Airplanes could not fly over mountains. They could not fly safely at night, and they had to land frequently to refuel. As for the flights themselves, they were uncomfortable, loud and bumpy. Since planes were nothing more than fabric-covered wooden frames, passengers had to stuff cotton in their ears to shut out the noise of the engines. And without a proper air circulation system, cabins reeked of motor oil, gasoline and the disinfectant used to clean up after airsick passengers. The only way to escape the smell was to open a window, which turned a plane's cabin into a wind tunnel. Despite all these inconveniences, however, plane travel grew from around 6,000 passengers in 1926 to 173,000 passengers in 1929.

Around 1930, airline companies began hiring "air stewardesses" in hopes of making their passengers more comfortable. These women (forerunners of our modern-day flight attendants) not only offered passengers water, a sandwich and gum to help relieve ear pain (cabins were not pressurized back then), but they also carried luggage, took tickets and tidied up the cabin after a flight. More important, they were all registered nurses, capable of providing medical care in emergencies. Remarked one passenger, "They make things so much more homey."

Still, air travel in the 1930s was limited to the wealthy and people who had an important reason to fly. After all, flying was four times as expensive as taking the train, and the only reason most people chose it was speed.

All that changed in 1936, when the DC-3 was introduced. It could fly coast-to-coast faster than any passenger plane before, and it offered comfort. The plane was fitted with upholstered chairs that swiveled toward or away from the windows. The cabin was

An early passenger plane, circa 1928.

CONTINUED ON PAGE 88

CONTINUED FROM PAGE 87

soundproofed (no more wind and engine noises) and ventilated (no more bad smells).

The introduction of the DC-3 is credited with increasing the number of airline passengers from around 474,000 in 1932 to 1,176,858 in 1939. And even though it would be several years before more people traveled by air than by train, Americans were growing comfortable with the idea of flight. As one TWA ad liked to remind the public, "Now we can all soar like Amelia."

The interior of the DC-3, 1936.

Amelia smiled. "Please don't be concerned," she said. "It just seems that I must try this flight. I've weighed it all carefully. With it behind me life will be fuller and richer. I can be content. Afterward it will be fun to grow old."

George knew his independent wife's mind was made up. He vowed "to do everything in my power to help."

A flight around the world required lots of preparation. A course had to be marked

This publicity photo shows George and Amelia studying a globe, as well as charts, in preparation for the world flight.

out. Maps had to be drawn. Weather reports had to be studied. And what type of equipment would Amelia need to take along? The Putnams' living room, recalled one friend, "was just completely covered . . . with things they were testing—compasses, parachutes, three different kinds of rubber rafts."

Starting in early 1936 (months before Amelia took possession of the Electra), George flung himself into the enormous task of obtaining permission for her to fly over or land in every country along her route. Additionally, he had to arrange for supplies of gasoline and oil at more than thirty points. Then he had to decide at which of these stops the plane would need to be overhauled. After all, the plane couldn't fly 27,000 miles

The Putnams invested their entire life's savings in the around-the-world flight. "I more or less mortgaged my future," Amelia admitted.

George agreed. "It is a gamble," he said. If his wife failed, they would be broke. But "if she succeeds, our financial futures are set."

Already, George had cut a deal with the *New York Herald-Tribune* for a syndicated column to be written by Amelia during the trip. He had lined up a lucrative lecture tour to start as soon as she returned. He'd even negotiated a book contract with Harcourt Brace. But his most interesting moneymaking scheme involved stamp covers.

In partnership with Gimbel's department store, George had 5,000 stamp covers (envelopes with commemorative markings) printed. These stamp covers were then offered to collectors for $5 apiece. They sold like hotcakes. Why? Because Amelia not only signed each cover, but she also promised to take them along on the flight.

Signing these stamp covers became a sort of game: ten autographs before her morning orange juice, fifteen before her bacon and eggs, twenty-

A stamp cover Amelia signed (and left behind) before her flight around the world.

five before bed. She was willing to do anything for this flight, and the sale of the stamp covers would defray a significant portion of the cost. (The Putnams stood to make $25,000 from the covers, about $250,000 nowadays.)

Perhaps this explains why Amelia chose to keep the 5,000 stamp covers in the Electra's nose cargo hold, even as she obsessed about carrying unnecessary weight. To lighten the plane, she would remove clothes, parachutes and even her Morse code key. But she never abandoned the stamp covers. When she disappeared, they went with her.

without lots of maintenance. Once he decided where the plane would be worked on, he had to send the necessary engine parts and mechanics to those places.

"I felt like a master magician and jigsaw puzzle juggler," said George.

Meanwhile, Amelia wrestled with the biggest logistical problem of her flight—the Pacific Ocean. She could not fly over its entire expanse nonstop. Somehow she needed to refuel. How? She had an idea, but it required some help from her friends the Roosevelts. In November 1936 she wrote:

> Dear Mr. President,
> Some time ago I told you and Mrs. Roosevelt a little about my

confidential plans for a world flight. . . . The chief problem is the jump westward from Honolulu. The distance thence . . . is 3900 miles. . . . With that in view, I am discussing with the Navy a *possible refueling in the air over Midway Island.* . . . Knowing your own enthusiasm for voyaging, and your affectionate interest in Navy matters, I am asking you to help me secure Navy cooperation—that is, if you think well of the project. If any information is wanted as to purpose, plans, equipment etc., Mr. Putnam can meet anyone you designate, any time, anywhere.

After reading the letter, President Roosevelt agreed to "do what we can."

Amelia, however, changed her mind. Rather than refueling in the air, she switched to the possibility of landing on Howland Island, a tiny island within flying range of both New Guinea and Hawaii. The problem was, Howland Island didn't have an airstrip.

Could the United States government build her one? Amelia asked President Roosevelt. PLEASE FORGIVE TROUBLESOME FEMALE FLYER FOR WHOM THIS HOWLAND ISLAND PROJECT IS KEY TO WORLD FLIGHT ATTEMPT, ran one of her telegrams to the White House.

Roosevelt came to her rescue. He authorized funds for the construction of an airstrip on Howland Island, then made sure it was built swiftly *and* secretly. After all, commented one Earhart biographer, "the American taxpayer—in the throes of the Great Depression—might not have understood the necessity of building an entire airport for one-time use by a private individual."

FALSE START

Amelia had decided to fly from east to west: from Oakland, California, to Hawaii to Howland Island to Australia to Arabia to Africa to Brazil, and then to Miami and home. She figured the trip would take about six weeks.

As the starting date for the world flight neared, tensions grew. Believing that his wife needed a good laugh, George decided to play a prank. One evening, while he and Amelia were dining with navigator Harry Manning, as well as mechanic Bo McKneely, George slipped away from the table and made a secret telephone call to the chief of police.

Later, as Amelia drove the others to the airport, she was pulled over for speeding.

She argued with the policeman. There weren't any speed-limit signs posted, she complained, and she needed to get to the airport. She had a plane to work on.

But the policeman refused to listen to her arguments. He dragged her—along with the others—to night court, where the judge gave Amelia a stern lecture on driving too fast. Then he turned to George. "Are you responsible for this woman?"

Straight-faced, George replied, "No, Your Honor. I'm just a relative and I disown her."

People in the courtroom laughed, and Amelia realized George had played a joke on her.

The judge (who George thought was in on the prank but who really wasn't) fined Amelia one dollar. As she swept off to the cashier to pay, the judge beckoned George to the bench. Was that lady really Amelia Earhart? he asked.

George assured him that she was.

"I thought you were trying to kid me all the time," replied the judge. He ordered the fine returned to Amelia.

George laughed and laughed.

But Amelia soon got her revenge. Although George regularly took airplanes, he still suffered from airsickness. "Flying makes me queasy," he once confessed to reporters. A week after his prank, George boarded a plane for New York. About an hour into the flight, the attendant brought him a brightly wrapped package from Amelia. Eagerly, George tore off the paper to find . . . a raw pork chop.

She had also carefully chosen a navigator. He was Harry Manning, an experienced sailor and licensed pilot, who took a three-month leave of absence from his duties as a sea captain to make the trip.

From Oakland, California, to Howland Island, a third man would also fly with them—Fred Noonan. Noonan, a licensed pilot who had worked as a navigator for Pan American Airways, was put aboard when it was discovered that Manning would need help with celestial navigation (determining location based on the stars and other celestial bodies).

"It appears," said Amelia in early 1937, "that I am ready."

Technical advisor Paul Mantz disagreed. He had spent hours training Amelia to fly her new plane. She was a quick study, but Mantz still worried. She was about to make the most dangerous flight of her life in a powerful, complicated

Amelia in the cockpit of the Electra. It measured 4'6" long by 4'6" wide by 4'8" high—a very cramped space for long flights.

airplane loaded with special equipment—various weight, altitude and engine monitors. None of Amelia's previous planes had been equipped with any of these instruments. "You need more practice," Mantz advised her.

She needed more practice with her radio equipment, too. Joseph Gurr, who had been hired to install the plane's communication system, was eager for Amelia to learn how to use her radio and direction-finding equipment. He wanted to show her how to tune the receivers and how to operate the transmitters; to teach her correct radio procedures and help her understand what her radio system could and could not do. But every time Gurr begged her to come for a lesson, she put him off. She was too busy, she said. Her schedule was full. Finally—just weeks before her departure—she turned up at the airport hangar. Relieved, Gurr assumed he had all day to teach her everything about her radio. But after only an hour, Amelia left for an appointment. Gurr was stunned. "We never covered actual operations such as taking a bearing with the direction finder, [or] even contacting another radio station," he recalled. This very brief lesson was Amelia's only formal instruction in the use of her communication system. And it would be her gravest mistake. Wrote one aviation expert, "The solution to Amelia's future communication problems was right at her fingertips—if only she had understood how her radio worked."

Despite all these concerns, on the afternoon of March 17, 1937, Amelia—along with Harry Manning, Fred Noonan and Paul Mantz—climbed into the Electra. Once the hatch was down, Mantz took over the throttles in the left-hand seat while Amelia handled the flight controls in the copilot's seat. Even though she had flown the Electra more than two dozen times, Mantz wanted to go over the flying process one last time. Wrote Amelia, "[We] carefully worked out the piloting technique of that start. It was a team-play takeoff."

As for Mantz (who planned to travel with Amelia only as far as Hawaii), he had plenty of last-minute advice. "Never jockey the throttle," he told her. "Use the rudder and don't raise the tail too quick."

Minutes later, the Electra roared down the field and rose slowly into the sky. "An excellent takeoff on a muddy runway," an official from the Bureau of Air Commerce later reported to the White House. He didn't know that the takeoff was really Mantz's.

Sixteen hours later, the Electra landed in Hawaii. "Smooth flying," Amelia recorded in her log book, "but the next leg will not be so easy."

The long Pacific hop to tiny Howland Island was next. This was, by far, the hardest part of the trip. Still, Amelia felt confident. Even though the coast guard cutter *Itasca* would be standing by at Howland Island to offer help, she didn't expect to need any. She figured that at the start of the trip, "when everyone was fresh," and with three fliers aboard (herself, Manning and Noonan), they wouldn't have any problems finding that tiny dot of land.

Amelia was eager to put this part of the journey behind her, but for some reason she delayed her departure for a day. This delay, the press was told, was due to bad weather. But navy reports later stated that the forecast was for "favorable flying conditions over the entire route." The real reason, according to Paul Mantz, was that Amelia was exhausted. She needed to rest before setting out on this most difficult leg of her trip.

At daybreak on March 20, Amelia took the throttle herself and prepared to take off. But as the Electra rolled down the runway, the unexpected happened. The plane's right wing appeared to drop. Amelia corrected by reducing power on the opposite engine, but the plane swung out of control. With a loud crack, the landing gear collapsed, and the Electra "slid on its belly amid a shower of sparks" before coming to a stop.

Quickly, Amelia shut down the engines, preventing a fire. Then she sat for a few stunned moments in the cockpit before crawling out the cabin door behind Manning and Noonan. "Something must have gone wrong," she said in a dazed voice.

It was a disastrous accident. The Electra's right wing, both engine housings, the main landing gear, the underside of the fuselage and both propellers were badly damaged. In Oakland, where George awaited word of his wife's takeoff, the phone rang. It was a reporter for one of the press associations. "Have you heard?" asked the reporter. "They crashed . . . the ship's in flames."

Recalled George, "I could not listen further." Handing the phone to a friend, "I moved out into the cold morning, trying to walk steadily. In a few minutes [people] came racing after me. 'No fire . . . no fire at all. . . . False report! No one hurt!'"

Immediately, George "shakily scribbled" a cable to his wife: SO LONG AS YOU AND THE BOYS OK THE REST DOESN'T MATTER AFTER ALL IT'S JUST ONE OF THOSE THINGS WHETHER YOU WANT TO CALL IT A DAY OR KEEP GOING LATER IS EQUALLY JAKE WITH ME.

An hour later, Amelia telephoned him. "Her voice weary with sadness," recalled George, "she said she wanted to try again."

Amelia and George returned home to California, where they decided to postpone the flight until May. The postponement cost them a crew member—Harry Manning. The reason released to the press was that Manning had to be back at his job. But Manning later said he quit because he had lost faith in Amelia's skill as a pilot and was fed up with her "bullheadedness." Whatever the reason, Manning's absence left Fred Noonan as sole navigator.

More important, Amelia was forced to change her course. Now she would have to fly west to east, because the later starting date meant that the weather patterns—storms and winds—would be different.

"Now everything must be worked out again," remarked George. "New maps and charts; new stores and gasoline and spare parts; new permissions and official documents and headaches for the husband."

SECOND ATTEMPT

On May 21, 1937, Amelia took off for Miami from Oakland on the first leg of her second world flight attempt. With her were George, Fred Noonan and Bo McKneely, a flight mechanic. As the three flew eastward across the country, they paid close attention to the plane's performance. "We planned to shake out any bugs in Florida," explained Amelia.

They spent a week in Miami while McKneely and other mechanics went over the plane. They tinkered with the fuel pumps and the landing gear. They also changed a radio antenna in hopes of increasing the distance it could transmit messages. George and Amelia, meanwhile, did a little sunbathing and went fishing on a friend's yacht.

On June 1, in the dark of early morning, Amelia, Fred and George drove to the airport. They loaded a small amount of luggage into the Electra, along with two thermoses of tomato juice. Then George and Amelia slipped into the hangar for a private goodbye. "There in the dim chill we perched briefly on cold concrete steps, her hands in mine," he recalled. "There is very little one says at such times."

When the mechanic called that all was ready, Amelia walked out to the airplane. "She seemed to me very small and slim and feminine," said George. Then Amelia and Fred climbed into the plane, and she started the ship's two engines. Amelia "exuded confidence and smiles," recalled one of the bystanders.

George "did not." Perhaps he was recalling his wife's words from the night before. "When I go," she had said, "I'd like best to go in my plane. Quickly."

George paced nervously back and forth on the tarmac until the silver plane disappeared into the sky. Ever after, he would remember his wife's eyes, "clear with the good light of the adventure that lay before her."

The SEARCH CONTINUES

WARNER THOMPSON, commander of *Itasca*, had spent the last three days piecing together the various reports of signals heard across the Pacific. He had followed up on these reports by ordering the cutter to search hundreds of miles of ocean. But *Itasca* had found nothing.

Now, on the morning of July 5, the navy radio station in Wailupe reported hearing a Morse code signal from Earhart, giving her position as 281 miles north of Howland Island. (Officials were still unaware that the Morse code sending key had been removed from the Electra.) Thompson immediately ordered the ship to steam to this previously unsearched location. He calculated they would arrive at "281 north" by nightfall.

Just before nine p.m., two lookouts on the deck saw "a distinct flare" arc up into the night sky. In the radio room, Leo Bellarts immediately sent a voice message on 3105: "EARHART FROM *ITASCA*. DID YOU SEND UP A FLARE? SEND UP ANOTHER IDENTIFICATION."

Seconds afterward, wrote Commander Thompson in a later report, "another green light appeared (25 witnesses)."

Bellarts sent another message: "EARHART FROM *ITASCA*. WE SEE YOUR FLARES AND ARE PROCEEDING TOWARD YOU."

A nearby naval radioman picked up on Bellarts's transmissions and forwarded the information to other commands. Soon the Hawaiian coast guard station was informing the San Francisco station, "*Itasca* sighted flares and proceeding toward them."

But at 281 north Howland, the sky and airwaves had fallen silent. The cutter steamed at reduced speed, sweeping and flashing its searchlights, hoping for some sign of a floating plane or a raft. They saw nothing.

By ten p.m., Commander Thompson began to believe that he had not seen flares after all. "It was a mistake, and the signals seen were probably heat lightning."

But it was too late to take back the news. The next morning, the *New York Herald-Tribune* headline blared: "Earhart Flares Sighted by Cutter." Other news outlets picked up the story, and soon, people across the world waited for the exciting details of Amelia's rescue. "We are anxious to see pictures of the search and rescue," one reporter wired Commander Thompson.

While *Itasca* continued to search the area, coast guard officials tried to clear up the night's confusion. "Reports were in error," they said over and over again. The entire event had turned into a national embarrassment for the coast guard.

On the evening of July 5, Commander Thompson and *Itasca* were relieved of their leading role in the Earhart search. The rescue now rested in the hands of the U.S. Navy.

Last Flight
1937

Amelia Earhart's Own Day-to-Day Story . . .

Flight Around the Equator

Amelia Earhart is going to fly the world's equator—she who first flew the Atlantic almost ten years ago, later flew it again alone, still later flew the Pacific and soloed the length and breadth of the United States.

The world has been flown a number of times. But never by a woman. Never around its equator. And never in an East-to-West continuous flight. She plans to begin her flight next Monday.

She will fly the world's full circumference. And not as a barnstorming adventure but as a practical test—a limit test—of all that is modern in scientific and aerial invention pitted against the longest world flight ever contemplated—27,000 miles of it.

Her story . . . in three hops over the Pacific, a swing across British New Guinea and Australia, a line across the Malay Peninsula, an arc through India and Arabia, a jump across Africa and another across the South Atlantic—her story, as it happens, as told by her, will appear only in the New York Herald-Tribune.

It will begin the day the Electra—her "flying laboratory"—glides out of Oakland and over the Golden Gate on its way to the longest continuous flight ever attempted by man —or woman.

The announcement of exclusive coverage of Amelia's 1937 flight, New York Herald-Tribune.

THE FIRST LEGS OF THE JOURNEY were easy ones. Amelia and Fred flew eight hours to San Juan, Puerto Rico. From there they headed to Venezuela and then to Dutch Guyana. Along the way, Amelia put the plane on automatic pilot. (This innovation had been developed in 1932 and had been used by Wiley Post a year later during his solo flight around the world.) From her cockpit, she looked out, marveling at the "vivid greens and the blue of the sea reaching fingerlike into the island." She also pulled out her notebook and began taking notes. The *New York Herald-Tribune* was paying her to write a series of articles about her adventures along the way. She kept a logbook, too. This she intended to send home from time to time in preparation for the book she had promised Purdue she would write.

She and Fred Noonan were becoming friends, too. She had not known Fred before the flight, having offered him the job as navigator based solely on Harry Manning's recommendation. But now, "little by little I came to know my shipmate's full story," she said. These conversations, however, could take place only when the fliers were on the ground. In the air, the noise from the engines was so loud that it was impossible to do anything but shout. For this reason, they communicated by writing notes. Popular legend has it that Fred remained in the rear cabin, attaching his notes to the end of a bamboo fishing pole, which he then passed up to her. In truth, he spent much of his time in the cockpit with her, clambering into the cabin only when he needed to spread open a chart.

After Dutch Guyana, Amelia and Fred flew on to Brazil, where they stopped for two days so the plane could be serviced before the long hop to Africa. Amelia took the opportunity to do her laundry. Eight days into the trip and "I was on my last shirt and had abandoned hope that the appearance of my slacks ever again would be respectable." Afterward, she and Fred "went tourist," walking, shopping and taking photographs.

Two days later they climbed into the sky once again and began their 1,900-mile journey to western Africa and the French colonial city of Dakar (in modern-day Senegal). The flight went smoothly most of the way. But as they approached the coast of Africa, a thick haze obscured their view. The situation could have been disastrous, but with "our usual good luck," Fred Noonan later wrote, "we barged through okay." The fliers ended up landing fifty miles north of Dakar in St. Louis, Senegal.

By the next morning, the fliers were back on course. They now faced the long air route across Africa—4,500 miles, with four scheduled stops. The first of these was El Fasher in Sudan. To get there, they flew low, following the Niger River. Along the way, they spotted a herd of hippopotami that "resented our presence," wrote Amelia. When they landed, it was so hot that the airport's ground crew waited to refuel the plane until the sun went down. An eight-foot-tall thorn hedge to keep out rhinos and lions surrounded the airfield.

Flying over Africa reminded Amelia of her childhood game of Bogie. "For me," she wrote, "the dreams of long ago had come true. Only, back in Atchison, our imaginary African treks were taken on camels and elephants. Who would have imagined I would actually journey by airplane?"

The Other Passenger in the Plane

Fred Noonan with Amelia in 1937.

336 change to 36°
Estimate 79 Miles to
Dakar from 8:36 PM
What - put no words

One of the many notes Fred handed to Amelia during the flight.

Fred Noonan liked adventure. He was born in Chicago in 1894, and at the age of fourteen, he ran away to sea. He rounded Cape Horn (surrounded by some of the most dangerous seas in the world) seven times in ten years, joined the British merchant marine during World War I and was torpedoed three times. In 1930, he headed to Weems School of Navigation in Annapolis, Maryland, where he learned to fly, as well as to navigate planes. That same year, he joined Pan American Airways as a navigation teacher.

But Fred needed more action than the classroom provided. He begged Pan Am to transfer him to the Pacific, and the company did. There he used his skills to map out the air routes to Hawaii, Midway, Wake Island and Guam. "If anyone knew the Pacific, Fred did," said one of his coworkers. Within the world of aeronautics, he was considered "a navigational genius."

But Fred had a big problem—he had begun drinking, perhaps due to the pressures of his job. "[He] was the best navigator when he was sober," recalled Fred's Pan Am boss, "but he was inclined to go on benders. . . . [Sometimes] before take-off, he'd have to be poured aboard the airplane."

Fred left Pan Am in December 1936. Rumors swirled that he'd been fired for drinking. Was it true? Fred never admitted it, but it was obvious his life was falling apart. Not only had he lost his career, but the following March, his wife of ten years divorced him. A week later he was involved in a serious car accident caused by his drinking.

Then Amelia—needing a world-class navigator—offered him a spot on her around-the-world trip. He seized the opportunity.

Did Amelia know about Noonan's problems?

"She knew [he] was a drinker," recalled Amelia's sister, Muriel, "but she forgave him for it. She felt she had a particular understanding of the problem."

Their fourth and final African stop was in Assab, in what is now Eritrea, where they took on hundreds of gallons of gasoline before heading to Karachi (then in India, now in Pakistan), some 2,000 miles away. This leg of the journey had to be flown nonstop, because officials in Saudi Arabia had refused permission for Amelia to land. But no matter. The flight passed without incident.

From Karachi, Amelia sent a brief note to George. "I wish you were here," she wrote. "So many things you would enjoy. . . . Perhaps some day we can fly together to some remote places of the world—just for fun."

From Karachi, Amelia and Fred flew to Calcutta, 1,390 miles away. As they flew along the mountain ridges, a huge flock of black eagles rose from their roosts. "They soared about us lazily, oblivious to the Electra and giving its pilot some very bad moments," reported Amelia. "How the birds managed to miss the plane, I do not know. I had never had such an experience, and hoped never to have such another."

By reversing the direction of her world flight, Amelia had hoped to miss the monsoon rains that strike India every summer. But in Calcutta it had rained all night, forcing the Electra to land on a sodden, muddy runway. Should she wait until the weather changed? Airport officials said no. More rain was coming. If she didn't leave right away, she would be stuck in Calcutta for who knew how long. So Amelia decided to quickly refuel and head immediately for Akyab (now Sittwe), in what was then Burma. "That takeoff was precarious," she wrote. "The plane clung for what seemed like ages to the heavy soil before the wheels finally lifted. . . ."

After a short stop in Akyab, they headed for Rangoon. Amelia thought they had "outflown the monsoons." But not long into the flight, they ran into a wall of water. Headwinds battered the plane, and the rain slashed down so hard, it peeled patches of paint off the wings. It was impossible to see. Only Fred's navigational skills stood between them and a terrible accident. "After two hours and six minutes of going nowhere, Fred's uncanny navigational skills managed to return us to the airport," wrote Amelia.

They tried for Rangoon again the next morning. This time they climbed above the clouds into bright sunlight. The sight caused Amelia to burst into a poem by Longfellow. "'The hooded clouds, like Friars, / Tell their beads in drops of rain,'" she recited at the top of her voice.

After Rangoon came Singapore, a flight of over twelve hundred miles. "It was made without a hitch," reported Amelia. Singapore was followed by a hop to Bandung, Java, in what was then called the Netherlands East Indies (modern-day Indonesia). Monsoon weather, as well as a necessary repair to the fuel regulator, forced the fliers to stay in Bandung for some days. Amelia used the time to rest; then, on June 27, the fliers took off for Port Darwin, Australia.

The long cross-ocean flights were coming up now. In Australia, the Electra was carefully looked over to make sure everything was in working order. One important repair was made to the radio direction finder. One of its fuses had blown. Mechanics replaced it, then ran a ground test. It worked.

Meanwhile, Amelia and Fred lightened the plane by sending home anything they didn't need. Every single item not essential to the flight (with the exception of those 5,000 stamp covers) was boxed and mailed home. Even Amelia's lucky elephant-toe bracelet was returned. "There must not be a spare ounce of weight left," she said.

"So big," answered Amelia when a reporter asked her how big Howland Island was.

At dawn on June 29, 1937, the fliers took off for Lae, New Guinea. For the next seven hours and forty-three minutes, they battled strong headwinds, finally arriving at three p.m.

"My Electra now rests on the edge of the Pacific," Amelia wrote that day in her journal. "Somewhere beyond the horizon lies home and California. Twenty-two thousand miles have been covered so far. There are 7,000 miles to go."

In Lae, the plane was once again serviced. Oil and oil filters were changed, spark plugs were cleaned

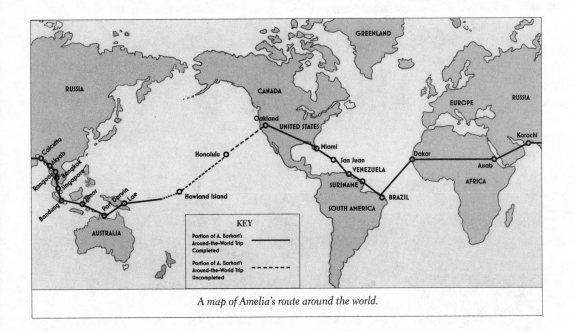

A map of Amelia's route around the world.

and the engines were checked. While this was being done, Amelia and Fred once again studied their maps and charts. Both fliers understood the difficulty of the task ahead of them. "[Howland Island] is such a small spot in the Pacific," she said, "I shall be glad when we have the hazards of its navigation behind us." As for Fred, he felt confident that he would have "no trouble finding the island."

With all preparations complete, the fliers climbed into the Electra. It was ten a.m. on July 2, 1937. For a moment Amelia listened to what she had earlier described as the engines' "full-throated smooth song." Then she taxied to the end of the runway. Seconds later they were in the air and on their way to Howland Island.

ALL SEARCH *for* EARHART TERMINATED

EVEN THOUGH it was no longer leading the search, *Itasca* continued to crisscross the waters near Howland Island for any sign of Amelia and Fred. Joining the cutter were a navy battleship, three destroyers, a sea plane tender and an aircraft carrier. But it was the U.S.S. *Colorado*, a battleship from Honolulu, that arrived first. Its orders were to search the Phoenix group—eight islands 350 miles south of Howland.

Aerial view of Gardner Island, where John Lambrecht claimed to have seen signs of recent habitation.

On the morning of July 9, all the U-3 spotter biplanes from the *Colorado* headed toward the first of the group, McKean Island. All they found were flocks of birds.

From McKean they continued to Gardner Island (now called Nikumaroro, in the Republic of Kiribati), sixty miles away. As the planes circled overhead, Senior Aviator Lieutenant John Lambrecht saw something that made him think someone might be down there. "Here signs of habitation were clearly visible," he wrote in his report. Unfortunately, he did not record what he saw. Instead, the planes circled and zoomed over the spot, but no one on the ground responded. "It was finally taken for granted that no one was there," he concluded.

Satisfied that Amelia had not landed on Gardner Island, the pilots moved on. "From Gardner," Lambrecht reported, "the planes headed southeast for Carondelet Reef, a good ten miles away." But the reef was under water. Finding nothing, the planes returned to the ship.

The next day they were back at it, continuing with a search of the Phoenix Islands. First was a flight to Sydney Island. "Upon dropping for inspection we could discover nothing which indicated the missing fliers had landed there," wrote

Lambrecht. From Sydney Island, they flew to Phoenix, Enderbury and Birnie—small, barren islands also in the Phoenix group that offered no clues.

At last they arrived at Canton Island (now known as Kanton or Abariringa), the largest in the chain. "It held the *Colorado*'s only remaining hope of finding Miss Earhart and her navigator alive," wrote Lambrecht. But the pilots came up empty-handed. That night the mood aboard the battleship was "disappointed and search weary."

Meanwhile, the military continued to closely monitor the airwaves for any signals from the lost plane. But Earhart's frequency had grown eerily silent. "We didn't hear anything but static," recalled radioman Leo Bellarts.

The search continued for another eight days. In all, the military covered 250,000 square miles and spent 4.9 million tax dollars (about $58 million nowadays). It was the biggest search ever undertaken by the United States. But as days passed, hope evaporated. "Facts must be faced," President Roosevelt finally said. At two minutes before five p.m. on July 18, 1937, an order was issued. It simply read: "All search for Earhart terminated."

Later

AMELIA LOST! This was the newspaper headline thousands of Americans woke up to on July 3, 1937. And for the next ten days the lost flier stayed on the front page as people grasped for any tidbit of information. They stayed glued to their radios and flocked to movie theaters to watch newsreel films showing ships and planes searching the expanse of the Pacific. "We are stunned," declared a Kentucky woman. As the days passed, newspapers, unsure about when to print an obituary, began running lengthy articles eulogizing the lost flier. And hundreds of Americans sent letters of consolation to Amelia's family.

Among them were these lines from a fifteen-year-old California girl: "I want to choke the Navy for not finding her. . . . I feel she is alive and I know she needs us."

In another letter, a New Jersey woman wondered, "How can she just be gone?"

And one aspiring female pilot from Oklahoma shared these feelings: "I have had people tell me I'm crazy to stay up all night listening to the radio about Amelia and they say Miss Earhart was nothing to me, but I loved Miss Earhart as if she were my own sister, because I know she is a kind and wonderful woman. There isn't another woman I worship more." Reading her words, recalled one family member, "practically reduced George to tears."

Unable to publish a eulogy, the Los Angeles Herald and Express *instead included this pictorial summary of Amelia's life, entitled "The World Remembers," in its July 13, 1937, issue.*

Distraught, he refused to leave the coast guard station in San Francisco. He simply stayed in the radio room, going days without sleep, waiting for news that his wife had been found. Those present remembered how he paced back and forth for hours, sweat running down his face. "A.E. will pull through," he told a reporter. "She has more courage than anyone I know."

As the hours and days wore on, George wracked his brain for possibilities, going over and over the sea charts. Had the navy searched the vicinity of the Phoenix Islands? he wondered. Could it be possible that, unable to find Howland Island, Amelia had turned back to the Gilbert Islands (now Kiribati)? Might her plane be afloat and drifting south?

George called navy and coast guard chiefs to request that ships be diverted from the organized search to follow up on his ideas. He even offered to pay for any additional costs involved in these searches. "George was a doer," recalled one friend. "It was impossible for him to retreat into helplessness."

He refused to quit even after the government abandoned the search. Weeks later, he was still following up on his own questions. He even flew to Washington, D.C., where he badgered anyone who would listen about continuing the search.

But it all came to nothing. Eventually, he was forced to face the sad truth—Amelia was dead. "I feel I have been running away from something I should have faced," he confessed to his mother-in-law. "Mostly, my days have been filled with an effort to keep from thinking. The total emptiness is appalling."

He kept busy by flinging himself into two new projects. The first was a book based on the notes Amelia had mailed from various stops on her world flight. Titled *Last Flight*, it was published in November 1937, and while it did not become a bestseller, sales were strong.

Sales for George's second project—a biography of Amelia—were also strong. Calling this book *Soaring Wings*, George delved into his wife's past by writing to friends and relatives for their stories and remembrances of her. His work—which first uncovered such often-told tales as the ones about little Amelia's backyard roller coaster and the hand-sewn bloomers she wore—became the basis of all future biographers' work.

"Even after her death," commented one friend, "he was still working for Amelia Earhart . . . still promoting her heroic image."

But no publicity scheme concocted by George Putnam could have enhanced Amelia's image more than her tragic accident. In life, she had been famous. But now—by vanishing—she became a legend. As the mystery of her disappearance gripped the public's imagination, rumors began to swirl.

It was whispered that Amelia had really been on a top-secret mission for the U.S. government. Her objective had been to fly over Japanese fortifications in the central Pacific, gathering important military information.

Was this true? When Amelia's mother asked the Roosevelts about the rumor, Eleanor said no. "We loved Amelia too much to send her to her death," she replied.

Another rumor speculated that a Japanese fishing boat had picked up Amelia and Fred after the fliers had

No Funeral

Because no body was ever found, Amelia Earhart was never given a funeral or memorial service. There were no national tributes or flags lowered to half-mast. Instead, on January 5, 1939—two years after her disappearance—this tiny paragraph appeared in the back pages of newspapers all across the country:

Amelia Earhart, noted woman flyer who disappeared on an around the world flight in the summer of 1937, was declared legally dead today. The action was taken at the request of the flyer's husband, George Palmer Putnam.

Flat-out Broke

Some people criticized George for profiting from his dead wife's name. "He must be making millions," remarked one newspaper editor. But in truth, George was broke. "For many years I had been pouring my fullest energy and thoughtfulness, and largely my income, into A.E.'s activities and ambitions," he wrote to his mother-in-law. "You know that the final tragedy, and its aftermath, deeply involved me financially. . . . For which . . . I have no regrets. If we had to do it again, I'd spend everything I had again."

When the bills related to Amelia's flight, as well as her search, began pouring in, George hunted for the means to pay them. But the book deals went only a small way toward clearing the debt. Eventually, he was forced to sell his Rye, New York, estate to keep from going bankrupt. Still, "the money was never important," said George, "considering the greater loss of my wife and friend." For the rest of his life, he suffered under the financial burden caused by the failed flight.

crash-landed off course. Since relations between Japan and the United States were strained at that time (war between the two countries broke out four years later), Earhart and Noonan were imprisoned on Saipan, where they eventually died.

Still another rumor suggested that Amelia, tired of all the publicity, faked her death, assumed an alias and moved to New Jersey.

Until his death in 1950, George worried that the mystery of her disappearance would overshadow Amelia's real legacy.

And what was Amelia's legacy?

Wrote biographer Mary S. Lovell, "[It] is the legend of an ordinary girl growing into an extraordinary woman who dared to attempt seemingly unattainable goals in a man's world."

It is impossible to gauge how much Amelia's life inspired the generations of women who came after her. At a time when women felt limited to the roles of wife and mother, she encouraged them to challenge themselves and seize their dreams. And she did it with zest, boldness and courage.

The letter Amelia left behind.

Amelia Earhart was not afraid of death. She had said so many times. A paragraph from a letter she left behind in case she did not return from her world flight proved that. She wrote:

> Please know I am quite aware of the hazards. I want to do it because I want to do it. Women must try to do things as men have tried. When they fail, their failure must be but a challenge to others.

As a grief-stricken Eleanor Roosevelt told reporters, "I am sure Amelia's last words were 'I have no regrets.'"

BIBLIOGRAPHY

In preparing to write this book, I was confronted by a mountain of research material, much of it drawn from a variety of primary documents housed in archival collections. These collections include:

The George Palmer Putnam Collection of Amelia Earhart Papers, Purdue University Library Special Collections, West Lafayette, Indiana, which houses 16.5 cubic feet of documents, including the flier's correspondence, creative writings, printed materials, scrapbooks and personalized belongings.

The Arthur and Elizabeth Schlesinger Library, Radcliffe College, Cambridge, Massachusetts, which includes documents saved by Muriel Earhart Morrissey (Amelia's sister), including baby books, school-related papers, genealogical papers and Amelia's "Activities of Women" scrapbook, as well as the Amy Otis Earhart oral collection.

The International Group for Historic Aircraft Recovery (TIGHAR) Earhart Collection, Wilmington, Delaware, which has amassed an impressive collection of primary documents from numerous places, including dozens of private collections, most of which pertain to the science of aerial navigation, as well as Earhart's disappearance, including *Itasca's* radio logbooks, oral histories from participants in the search and even video footage of Earhart's last takeoff from Lae, New Guinea.

In addition to these archival collections, Earhart's published works were particularly helpful. These included:

"Flying the Atlantic and Selling Sausages Have a Lot in Common." *American Magazine*, August 1932, pp. 13–35.

"A Friendly Flight Across the Country." *New York Times Magazine*, July 19, 1931, pp. 27–34.

The Fun of It: Random Records of My Own Flying and of Women in Aviation. New York: Brewer, Warren and Putnam, 1932.

Last Flight. New York: Harcourt Brace and Company, 1937.

"My Flight from Hawaii." *National Geographic*, vol. 65, no. 5, May 1935, pp. 593–609.

20 Hrs., 40 Min.: Our Flight in the Friendship. Washington, D.C.: National Geographic Adventure Classics, 2003.

"Women's Status in Aviation." *Sportsman Pilot*, March 1929, unpaged.

Providing a different perspective on historic events, as well as adding to my understanding of Earhart's marital relationship, were these books written by her husband, George Palmer Putnam:

Wide Margins: A Publisher's Autobigraphy. New York: Harcourt, Brace and Company, 1942.

Soaring Wings: A Biography of Amelia Earhart. New York: Harcourt, Brace and Company, 1939.

Family members and friends also left behind numerous reminiscences of Earhart. Most useful were:

Backus, Jean, ed. *Letters from Amelia, 1901–1937*. Boston: Beacon Press, 1982.

Morrissey, Muriel Earhart. *Courage Is the Price: The Biography of Amelia Earhart*. Wichita, Kan.: McCormick-Armstrong, 1963.

—— "The Reminiscences of Muriel Earhart Morrissey," 1960, Oral History Collection of Columbia University, New York.

—— and Carol L. Osborne. *Amelia, My Courageous Sister: Biography of Amelia Earhart*. Santa Clara, Calif.: Osborne Publisher, Incorporated, 1987.

Nichols, Ruth. *Wings for Life*. Philadelphia: J. B. Lippincott Co., 1957.

Smith, Elinor. *Aviatrix*. New York: Harcourt Brace Jovanovich, 1981.

Southern, Neta Snook. *I Taught Amelia to Fly*. New York: Vantage Press, 1974.

Helping me grasp the role of women in aviation, as well as Earhart's place in early-twentieth-century America, were:

Lovell, Mary S. *The Sound of Wings*. New York: St. Martin's Press, 1989.

Samuelson, Lt. Col. Nancy B., U.S.A.F. "Equality in the Cockpit: A Brief History of Women in Aviation." *Air University Review*, May–June 1984.

Ware, Susan. *Still Missing: Amelia Earhart and the Search for Modern Feminism*. New York: W. W. Norton & Company, 1993.

For the newest scholarship on Earhart's disappearance and the often contradictory facts surrounding the search effort, as well as a clear understanding of communication and navigation techniques and technologies of the 1930s, I relied on these works:

"An Answering Wave: Why the Navy Didn't Find Amelia." *Naval Institute Proceedings*, February 1993.

Brandenburg, Bob. "Analysis of Radio Direction Finder Bearings in the Search for Amelia Earhart." *TIGHAR*, August 2006.

——"Harmony and Power: Could Betty Have Heard Amelia Earhart on a Harmonic?" *TIGHAR*, August 2006.

Carey, James. "Diary of UH Student on Hunt for Amelia Earhart Tells Minute-by-Minute How Tragic News Came." *Ka Elele O Hawaii* [the University of Hawaii newspaper], July 29, 1937, pp. 1–3.

Cooper, Daniel. U.S. Army Report: "Expedition to the American Equatorial Islands in Connection with Amelia Earhart Flight," July 27, 1937. National Archives, RG 94/407, file 581-81.

Gillespie, R. *Finding Amelia: The True Story of the Earhart Disappearance*. Annapolis, Md.: Naval Institute Press, 2006.

Thompson, Warner. U.S. Treasury Department Report: "Cruise Report, 4 June to 24 July, 1937—embracing Earhart Flight & Equatorial Island Cruise," Naval Historical Center, RG 26.

—— U.S. Treasury Department Report: "Radio Transcripts—Earhart Flight," July 19, 1937, National Archives, RG 26.

Other invaluable sources have been cited within the notes to the chapters in which they were used.

FINDING AMELIA ON THE WEB

www.tighar.org

You can read the original transcripts of Amelia's last radio transmissions, peruse *Itasca*'s logbook and even watch actual film footage of Amelia's last takeoff from Lae, New Guinea. This Web site is loaded with lots of other information too, including all of Betty Klenck's notebook, scholarly and scientific articles about Earhart's disappearance and a video about TIGHAR's archaeological expeditions. By far the best Web site about Amelia's disappearance, it also includes much information about her life and career.

http://earchives.lib.purdue.edu

Much of Purdue's Earhart archive has been digitized and can be viewed at this site. Diaries, letters, photographs, manuscript pages and much more are available.

www.acepilots.com/earhart.html

Basic facts and photographs about Earhart's childhood, her life as an aviator, her last flight and her disappearance can be found here.

www.museumofwomenpilots.com

This site is devoted to the history of women pilots and includes photos and biographies of Earhart and her fellow Women's Air Derby contestants.

www.britannica.com/EBchecked/topic/175680/amelia-earhart

Watch a clip from one of the newsreels that movie audiences would have seen during the search in 1937.

SOURCE NOTES BY CHAPTER

JULY 2, 1937—THE MORNING HOURS. Earhart's radio broadcasts: *Itasca* radio logs; July 1–2, 1937, TIGHAR Collection; Thompson "Radio Transcripts"; Bellarts's response: Leo G. Bellarts, transcript of interview, April 11, 1973, TIGHAR Collection. **Call Letters:** Gillespie. **The Way It Works:** Gillespie.

LITTLE AMELIA. Earhart's threads: Earhart *Fun*. **Baby Earhart:** Amelia Earhart Baby Book, Schlesinger Library, Radcliffe College, Cambridge, Mass.; Morrissey *Courage*. **Life in Atchison:** Earhart *20 Hrs*. and *Fun*; Putnam *Soaring Wings*, Morrissey *Courage*. **School Days:** Earhart *Fun*; Morrissey "Reminiscences"; Schlesinger Library, Radcliffe College. **Amelia Earhart, Poet:** Schlesinger Library, Radcliffe College. **Life in Kansas City:** Morrissey *Courage*; Morrissey and Osborne. **Bloomers!:** Earhart *Fun*. **What a Ride!:** Lovell. **Changes:** Earhart *Fun*.

JULY 2, 1937—THE DAY WEARS ON. Commander Thompson's decision: Thompson "Radio Transcripts" and "Cruise Report"; Gillespie; Bellarts interview. **Morse Code:** *Your Introduction to Morse Code*, Newington, Conn.: American Radio Relay League, July 1, 2001.

FAMILY SECRET. Early Days in Des Moines: Morrissey *Courage*; Lovell. **Dad's Sickness:** Morrissey *Courage* and "Reminiscences"; Backus. **Lean Years:** Morrissey and Osborne; Schlesinger Library, Radcliffe College. **Separation:** Morrissey *Courage*; Earhart *Fun*; Lovell.

JULY 2, 1937—MABEL'S STORY. Mabel Larremore's story: Gillespie. **Radio 101:** Gillespie.

FINDING HERSELF. Ogontz: Earhart *Fun*; "Activities of Women" scrapbook, Schlesinger Library, Radcliffe College. **First Urge to Fly:** Lovell; Ware; Earhart *Fun*; Morrissey "Reminiscences." **A Brief History of Flight:** R. G. Grant, *Flight: 100 Years of Aviation*, New York: DK Adult, 2002. **Back in the States:** Earhart *Fun*.

JULY 3, 1937—AN UNUSUAL OFFER. Hawaiian radio station's offer: Gillespie.

FIRST FLIGHT. Amelia's first meet: Earhart *Fun* and *20 Hrs*.; Morrissey *Courage*; Putnam *Soaring Wings*. **Danger!:** Paul F. Collins, *Tales of an Old Air-faring Man: A Half Century of Incidents, Accidents, and Providence*, Stevens Point, Wisc.: University of Wisconsin Stevens Point Press, 1983. **Fledgling Flyer:** Southern; Earhart *Fun* and *20 Hrs*; Lovell; Ware; Samuelson. Neta Snook: Southern. **A Short Cut:** Morrissey and Osborne. **A Few Flying Lessons from Amelia:** Earhart *Fun*. **Grounded:** Earhart *Fun* and *20 Hrs*.; Putnam *Soaring Wings*; Backus. **A Little Romance:** Morrissey and Osborne.

JULY 3, 1937—VOICES IN THE NIGHT. *Itasca* radio logs, July 3, 1937; Thompson "Radio Transcripts"; Gillespie.

FAME. Charles Lindbergh and other Atlantic-crossing attempts: Edward Jablonski, *Atlantic Fever*, New

York: Macmillan, 1972. **Enter George Putnam:** Putnam *Wide Margins* and *Soaring Wings*; Lovell; Ware. **Opportunity Comes Calling:** Earhart *20 Hrs.* and *Fun*; Putnam *Wide Margins*; Hilton H. Railey, *Touch'd with Madness*, New York: Carrick & Evans, 1938. **Preparations:** Earhart *20 Hrs.*; Putnam *Wide Margins*; Obituary of Wilmer Stultz, *New York Times*, July 2, 1929, p. 16; Amelia Earhart will dated May 20, 1928, Amelia Earhart Collection, Seaver Center for Western History Research, Natural History Museum of Los Angeles County, California; Morrissey *Courage*. **In Flight:** Earhart *20 Hrs.*; Putnam *Soaring Wings*; "Boston Girl Starts Atlantic Hop," *New York Times*, June 4, 1928, pp. 1, 3–4; "Amelia Earhart Flies Atlantic," *New York Times*, June 19, 1928, p. 1. **Celebrity:** Ware; Samuelson; Lovell; Putnam *Wide Margins* and *Soaring Wings*; **Earhart Enterprises:** Ware; Putnam *Soaring Wings*; **Amelia's Little Plane:** Backus.

JULY 4, 1937—DANA'S STORY. Gillespie.

VAGABONDING, RECORD BREAKING AND ROMANCE. **Cross-Country Flight:** Earhart Fun and "Friendly Flight Across the Country"; Putnam *Soaring Wings*. **Race!:** Smith; Nichols; Judy Lomax, *Women of the Air*, New York: Dodd, Mead, 1987. **Not Very Nice:** Smith; Lovell. **What Next?:** Lovell; Backus; Morrissey and Osborne. **Was It Love?:** Magazine clipping, Special Collections Library, Purdue University, Scrapbook #8, believed to be from *The Illustrated Love Magazine*, January 1932, pp. 25–27; Putnam *Wide Margins*; Earhart "Flying the Atlantic." **Alone in the Night Sky:** Earhart Fun; Putnam *Soaring Wings*; "Miss Earhart Tells the Prince All About It," [London] *Daily Express*, May 29, 1932, pp. 4–12; "Amelia Denies Flying Atlantic Takes Courage," *Daily Tribune*, June 4, 1932, p. 2; "Mrs. Putnam's Four Leaves of Laurel," *Literary Digest*, June 4, 1932, pp. 5–15. **What Did Amelia Eat?:** Spe ech clipping, Purdue Special Collections, Scrapbook #8 for 1935, undated. **Awards!:** Lovell. **Special Friends:** Ware; Irene Juno, "In the Air with Our Flying First Lady," *Good Housekeeping*, vol. 96, June 1933, pp. 26–27, 162; Marion Perkins, "Who Is Amelia Earhart?" *Survey Graphic*, July 1, 1928, p. 393. **More Challenges:** George Palmer Putnam, "The Forgotten Husband," *Pictorial Review*, December 1932, pp. 16–34; "Lesser Halves of Famous Wives," *New York World-Telegram*, February 8, 1932, pp. 12–14; Earhart *Last Flight* and "My Flight from Hawaii"; "Mexico–New York Record Set by Miss Earhart," *Oakland Tribune*, May 9, 1935, p. 4. **A Radio First:** Earhart "My Flight from Hawaii"; George Palmer Putnam, "A Flyer's Husband," *The Forum*, June 1935, pp. 330–32. **Paid Stunt or Heroic Adventure?:** Magazine clipping, Purdue Special Collections, Scrapbook #12, *Newsweek*, January 19, 1935; Leslie Ford, "A Flier in Sugar," *The Nation*, vol. 140, no. 3630, January 30, 1935, p. 21; "A Useless Adventure," *The Aeroplane*, January 16, 1935, p. 6.

JULY 5, 1937—BETTY'S STORY. Betty Klenck's notebook, TIGHAR Collection; Bradenburg "Harmony and Power"; Gillespie.

PLANS. Ruth W. Freehaufer, *R. B. Stewart and Purdue University*, West Lafayette, Ind.: Purdue University Press, 1983; Earhart *Last Flight*; Putnam *Soaring Wings*; Ware; Samuelson; Helen Welshimer, "Amelia Turns Career Pilot," *EveryWeek* magazine, May 17, 1936, unpaged. **Science or a Racket?:** Lovell. **A New Adventure:** Earhart *Last Flight*; Gillespie; Amelia Earhart to President Roosevelt, January 8, 1937, Purdue Special Collections; Putnam *Soaring Wings*. **Flying the Friendly Skies:** Henry Ladd Smith, *Airways: The History of Commercial Aviation in the United States*, New York: Alfred A. Knopf, 1942. **Other Arrangements:** Ware. **Pranks!:** Lovell. **False Start:** "Story of 'Dream' Come True Told by Miss Earhart, Starting Flight," *New York Herald-Tribune*, March 18, 1937, p. 1; Gillespie; "Eyewitness Report of George Miller and Others to the Official Board of Inquiry," March 23, 1937, U.S. Navy Archives, Exhibits C–F; Fred Goerner, *The Search for Amelia Earhart*, New York: Doubleday, 1966. **Second Attempt:** Gillespie; Ware; Earhart *Last Flight*.

JULY 5–6, 1937—THE SEARCH CONTINUES. Thompson "Cruise Report"; Bellarts interview; Carey; Gillespie.

LAST FLIGHT. Earhart *Last Flight*; Putnam *Soaring Wings*; in-flight note from Fred Noonan to Amelia

Earhart, Purdue Special Collections; Ann Holtgren Pellegreno, *World Flight: The Earhart Trail*, Ames, Ia.: Iowa State University Press, 1971; Gillespie; assorted cables from Amelia Earhart to *New York Herald-Tribune* offices, June 1–June 31, 1937, Purdue Special Collections. **The Other Passenger in the Plane:** Lovell.

JULY 7–18, 1937—ALL SEARCH FOR EARHART TERMINATED. Carey; "An Answering Wave"; Cooper; Gillespie.

LATER. Eleanor Roosevelt, "My Day," *New York Telegraph*, July 7, 1937, p. 16; Lovell; Ware; George Putnam to Amy Otis Earhart, May 9, 1939, Ref: 83-M69, Schlesinger Library, Radcliffe College. George Putnam to Amy Otis Earhart, December 3, 1939, Ref: 83-M69, Schlesinger Library, Radcliffe College; Putnam *Wide Margins* and *Soaring Wings*. **No Funeral:** Lovell. **Flat-out Broke:** Lovell.

PICTURE CREDITS

Many thanks to the organizations and people cited for their generous contributions.

Ames Historical Society: 35

Atchison County Historical Society: 11

Bettmann/Corbis: 8 (bottom), 55

The Hall of Fame of the Air: 78 (bottom)

Library of Congress: 17, 25, 29 (bottom), 30, 47, 52 (top), 57 (bottom), 102

National Air and Space Museum, Smithsonian Institution: 87, 88 (top)

National Archives and Records Administration: 8 (top), 59 (right-hand photograph in left column)

The Ninety-Nines, Inc., International Organization of Women's Pilots: 40

Purdue University, from Purdue University Libraries' George Palmer Putnam Collection of Amelia Earhart Papers: front jacket, 3, 32, 36, 38, 43, 50, 52 (bottom), 56, 57 (top), 58, 59 (right column), 60, 66, 67, 69, 72 (top), 75 (bottom), 78 (top), 84, 88 (bottom), 98, 100, 107, 110

Eric Rohmann: 45, 73, 103

Franklin D. Roosevelt Presidential Library and Museum: 76

Seaver Center for Western History Research, Natural History Museum of Los Angeles County: 72 (bottom)

Smithsonian National Postal Museum: 89

Schlesinger Library, Radcliffe Institute for Advanced Study, Harvard University: 7, 8 (middle), 9, 13, 18, 19, 22, 29 (top), 42, 75 (top)

TIGHAR Collection: 1, 2, 62, 80, 81, 92, 104

Page numbers in *italics* refer to illustrations.

funky
chunky
crocheted accessories

funky
chunky
crocheted accessories

jan eaton

Martingale®
& COMPANY

Conceived and produced by
Breslich & Foss Ltd., London

Volume © Breslich & Foss Ltd., 2006
Text: **Jan Eaton**
Photography: **Martin Norris**
Design: **Elizabeth Healey**
Project Management: **Janet Ravenscroft**

First American edition published by
Martingale & Company
20205 144th Ave. NE
Woodinville, WA 98072-8478 USA
www.martingale-pub.com

Martingale®
& C O M P A N Y

Printed in China

11 10 09 08 07 06   6 5 4 3 2 1

Library of Congress Cataloging-in-
Publication Data is available upon request.

ISBN: 1-56477-648-4

....

Mission Statement
*Dedicated to providing quality products and
service to inspire creativity.*

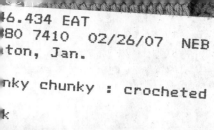

contents

introduction

In this book, you will discover how to turn five easy-to-make crochet patterns into over 60 delightfully individual accessories. By combining edgings, fastenings, and a wide range of embellishments with chunky crochet, you can make items that are truly unique.

Begin by checking out the Basic Techniques section on pages 8 to 23. Here you'll find all the information you need to take up the craft of crochet and become accustomed to choosing yarn and working with a crochet hook. Each technique is presented in an easy-to-understand sequence of instructions illustrated with close-up photographs that will encourage you every step of the way.

Once you've become familiar with basic crochet skills, it's time to move on and begin working the basic patterns on pages 24 to 29. Whether you want to crochet a scarf, bag, hat, pair of slippers, or mittens, you'll find these basic accessories are simple to make. If you're a newcomer to the craft of crochet but can handle making a foundation chain and working the basic stitches, you're ready to make your first scarf. As your skills and confidence improve with practice, try the bag and hat. When you are more proficient, make the slippers and mittens.

When you have mastered the basics, turn to the next chapters and discover how to adapt

accessories so they truly suit your style. Drawing on a wealth of decorative ideas and suggestions, there are over 60 inspiring accessories based around the five basic patterns. To make it easy to find your way around the book, the designs are divided into three sections. Edgings and Trimmings (pages 30 to 53), shows you how to craft different types of edgings and trimmings including fringes, ruffles, edging variations, pockets, flower trims, and tassels. Fastenings and Handles (pages 54 to 75), shows you how to make and attach different styles of handles and fastenings including grab handles, crochet buttons, earflaps, braids, sporty tabs, and toggle fastenings. Beading and Embellishing (pages 76 to 97), adds sparkle and glitz with beads, jewels, bells, and charms. We show you how to crochet beads into your work, and how to decorate crochet fabric with embellishments.

The final chapter, Customizing Crochet (pages 98 to 117) contains inspiring suggestions and helpful hints for exploring the boundaries of crochet to make something different. This chapter shows you how to improvise your own variations of the basic patterns, how to add stripes and different stitch patterns to your accessories, and how to work with novelty yarns. It also covers easy washing-machine felting, working surface crochet, and using recycled materials.

At the back of the book, starting on page 118, you'll find the illustrated Gallery which contains a photograph of every accessory and variation in the book. The designs are arranged by subject so that accessories of all the same type are shown together. We hope you will be inspired by our designs to customize the basic accessories to fit your own unique style.

jan eaton

chapter 1
basic techniques and patterns

This introductory section contains everything you need to know to get started in the craft of crochet and make your own **personalized accessories**. From **choosing** and handling yarns and crochet hooks to **blocking** finished pieces, and from **joining** a new yarn to making up the accessories, all the essentials are shown here in clear step-by-step photographs. Once you have mastered the art of working crochet stitches, turn to the **Basic Patterns on page 24**. Here you'll find instructions for making the Scarf, Buttonhole Bag, Hat, Slippers, and Mittens.

Materials

A crochet hook, a ball of chunky yarn, and a basic sewing kit are all you need to get started with this fascinating craft. Yarn and hooks come in a range of different weights, materials, and sizes and the information in this section will help you choose which to buy.

YARN

All the projects in this book can be made with your own choice of yarn colors and fiber composition. Many crocheters prefer pure wool yarns, but there are times when synthetic yarns may be preferable, such as for items that require frequent washing. Wool yarns may be more expensive than wool/synthetic blends and those made entirely from synthetics. You may prefer to use a pure cotton or synthetic/cotton blend yarn as these are less itchy than some made from wool.

Be adventurous and incorporate textured yarns, such as eyelash, tweed, or ribbon yarn in your accessory, but try to combine yarns of similar weight. As well as chunky weight yarns, you can use finer weights and crochet with two or more strands held together to make a thicker yarn. To make up a chunky yarn weight, try combining the following:

Each sample: one strand of chunky weight yarn

Left to right: One strand of worsted weight plus one sport weight; three strands of sport weight; two samples of two strands of double knitting

Left to right: Two strands of ribbon; one strand of plain double knitting, one strand of space-dyed double knitting; one strand of worsted weight, one strand of ribbon; one strand of double knitting, one strand of of novelty yarn

HOOKS

Crochet hooks are made from aluminum, wood, bamboo, plastic, or resin and come in a range of sizes from small (US size B/2.25 mm) to large (US size S/19 mm) to suit different weights of yarn. Smaller steel hooks are used to work very fine crochet in cotton thread. Choose whichever type of hook is comfortable to use.

Useful yarn/hook combinations

Sport weight (4ply)
US sizes B–E (2.25–3.5 mm)

Double knitting (DK)
US sizes F and G (3.75 and 4.5 mm)

Worsted weight (Aran)
US sizes H and I (5 mm and 5.5 mm)

Chunky weight (Chunky)
US sizes I–L (5.5–8 mm)

CROCHET EQUIPMENT
Yarn needles

Sewing needles with blunt tips and large eyes are available in a range of sizes to suit different yarn weights. Yarn needles may be straight or have bent tips.

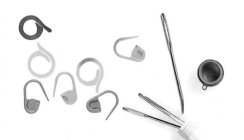

Row counter

A row counter is useful for keeping track of the number of rows you work.

Split ring stitch markers

Slip one of these onto your crochet to mark your place. Slip markers into a foundation chain at regular intervals to help you keep an accurate count.

Tape measure

Fiberglass tapes are best as they do not stretch. Buy one that has both imperial and metric measurements.

Scissors

Buy a small pair with sharp points. If you keep scissors in your work bag, buy a pair with a sheath.

Pins

Glass or plastic-headed pins are easy to see and don't slip through crocheted fabric. Also available are extra long marking pins.

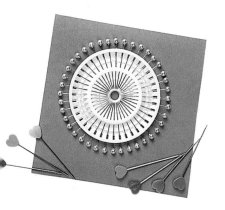

Holding the hook and yarn

There is no right or wrong way to hold the yarn and hook when you are crocheting: experiment until you find the most comfortable method. Hold the hook like a pen or overhand like a knife in your right hand and control the yarn with your left hand by feeding it through and around your fingers. (If you are left handed, simply reverse the information in this section.)

HOLDING THE HOOK

1

2

1 The most common way to handle a hook is to hold it like a pen. Center the tips of your right thumb and forefinger over the flat section of the hook.

2 Another way to hold the hook is to grasp the flat section between your right thumb and forefinger as if you were holding a knife.

HOLDING THE YARN

To control the yarn supply, loop the short end of the yarn over your left forefinger and take the yarn coming from the ball loosely around the ring finger on the same hand to tension it. Use your middle finger to help hold the work as you crochet. If it feels more comfortable, tension the yarn around your little finger instead.

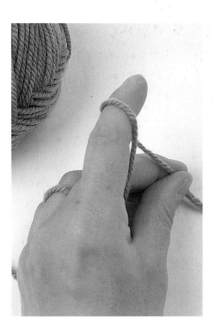

Starting to crochet

The first step when starting to crochet is to make a chain of the number of stitches given in the pattern, beginning with a slip knot. This is called the foundation chain and the first row of stitches is worked into it. There are different ways of inserting the hook into the chains and each produces a different kind of edge.

front   back

MAKING A SLIP KNOT

All types of crochet begin by making a slip knot to anchor the end of the yarn. Make the knot with your fingers, then slip it onto the hook.

1 With about 6 in. (15 cm) of the end of the yarn on the left, loop the yarn around your right forefinger. Carefully slip the loop off your finger. Holding the loop in your right hand, push a loop of the short end of the yarn through the first loop.

2 Insert the hook into the second loop. Gently pull the short end of the yarn to tighten the loop around the hook and complete the slip knot.

WORKING THE FOUNDATION CHAIN

The foundation chain is the crochet equivalent of casting on in knitting and it's important to make the required number of chains for the pattern you are going to follow.

1 Holding the hook with the slip knot in your right hand and the yarn in your left, wrap the yarn over the hook. This is known as "yarn over" or "yarn over hook" and you should always wrap the yarn over the hook in this way.

2 Draw the yarn through to make a new loop and complete the first stitch of the chain.

3 Repeat this step, drawing a new loop of yarn through the loop on the hook until the chain is the required length. Move up the thumb and finger of the hand that is grasping the chain after every few stitches to keep the tension even.

COUNTING CHAINS

The front of the chain looks like a series of V shapes or little hearts, while the back of the chain forms a distinctive "bump" of yarn behind each V shape. Count the stitches on either the front or back of the chain (whichever you find easier), counting each chain as one stitch, except for the chain on the hook, which is not counted.

1

2

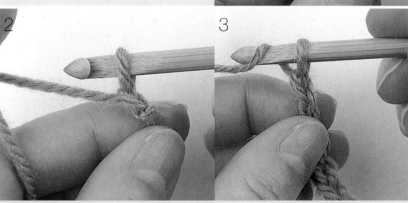
2   3

1

WORKING INTO THE FOUNDATION CHAIN

You're now ready to work the first row of stitches into the chain. The hook can be inserted into different places on the chain, but this is the easiest method for the beginner to use, although it results in a rather loose edge.

1 Holding the chain with the front facing you, insert the hook into the top loop of the chain and work the first stitch as stated in the pattern.

2 To make a stronger, neater edge, turn the chain so the back of it is facing you. Work the first row of stitches as instructed in the pattern, inserting the hook through the "bump" at the back of each chain stitch.

Tip

If you find it difficult to work the first row of stitches into the foundation chain because the chains are too tight, try using a hook one size larger to work the chain. Switch to the hook size suggested in the pattern after you've worked the chain.

TURNING CHAINS

When working crochet in rows or rounds, you will need to work a specific number of extra chains at the beginning of each row or round. The extra chains are needed to bring the hook up to the correct height for the particular stitch you will work next. When the work is turned at the end of a straight row, these extra chains are called a "turning chain," and when they are worked at the beginning of a round, they are called a "starting chain."

The list in the box (right) shows the correct number of chain stitches needed to make a turn for each type of stitch. If you are inclined to work chain stitches very tightly, you may find that you need to work an extra chain in order to prevent the edges of your work from becoming too tight.

> **Single crochet stitch:**
> 1 turning chain
>
> **Half double crochet stitch:**
> 2 turning chains
>
> **Double crochet stitch:**
> 3 turning chains

The turning or starting chain is usually counted as the first stitch of the row, except when working single crochet where the single turning chain is ignored. For example, "ch 3 (counts as 1 dc)" at the beginning of a row or round means that the turning or starting chain contains three chain stitches and these are counted as the equivalent of one double crochet stitch. A turning or

starting chain may be longer than the number required for the stitch and in that case, counts as one stitch plus a number of chains. For example, "ch 5 (counts as 1 dc, ch 2)" means that the turning or starting chain is the equivalent of one double crochet stitch plus two chain stitches.

At the end of the row or round, the final stitch is usually worked into the turning or starting chain worked on the previous row or round. The final stitch may be worked into the top chain of the turning or starting chain or into another specified stitch of the chain. For example, "1 dc into 3rd of ch-3" means that the final stitch is a double crochet stitch and it is worked into the third stitch of the turning or starting chain.

WORKING A SLIP STITCH

Slip stitch is rarely used to create a crochet fabric on its own. Instead, it is used to join rounds of crochet and to move the hook and yarn across a group of existing stitches to a new position.

1 To work a slip stitch into the foundation chain, insert the hook from front to back under the top loop of the second chain from the hook.

2 Wrap the yarn over the hook and draw it through both the chain and the loop on the hook. One loop remains on the hook and 1 slip stitch has been worked.

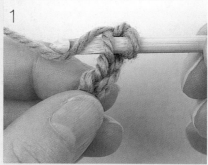

WORKING A SINGLE CROCHET STITCH

Single crochet is the shortest crochet stitch and it makes a firm, sturdy fabric with a dense texture. It needs pressing or blocking well (pages 22–23) as the fabric has a tendency to curl upward at the edges.

1 Work the foundation chain and insert the hook from front to back under the top loop of the second chain from the hook. Wrap the yarn over the hook and draw it through the first loop, leaving 2 loops on the hook.

2 To complete the stitch, wrap the yarn over the hook and draw it through both loops on the hook. Continue in this way along the row, working 1 single crochet stitch into each chain.

3 At the end of the row, work 1 chain for a turning chain (remember this chain does not count as a stitch) and turn the work.

4 Insert the hook from front to back under both loops of the first single crochet stitch at the beginning of the row. Work a single crochet stitch into each stitch of the previous row.

5 Work the final single crochet stitch into the last stitch of the row below, but not into the turning chain.

WORKING A HALF DOUBLE CROCHET STITCH

Halfway in height between single and double crochet, half double crochet makes a firm fabric with slightly more elasticity than single crochet. The fabric has horizontal ridges on both front and back.

1 Wrap the yarn over the hook before inserting it into the work.

2 Insert the hook from front to back into the work. (If you are at the beginning of the row, insert the hook under the top loop of the third chain from the hook.)

3 Draw the yarn through the chain, leaving 3 loops on the hook.

4 Wrap the yarn over the hook and draw it through all 3 loops on the hook. One loop remains on the hook and 1 half double crochet stitch has been worked.

5 Continue along the row, working 1 half double crochet stitch into each chain. At the end of the row, work 2 chains for the turning chain and turn the work.

6 Skipping the first half double crochet stitch at the beginning of the row, wrap the yarn over the hook, insert the hook from front to back under both loops of the second stitch on the previous row, and work a half double crochet stitch into each stitch made on the previous row.

7 At the end of the row, work the last stitch into the top stitch of the turning chain.

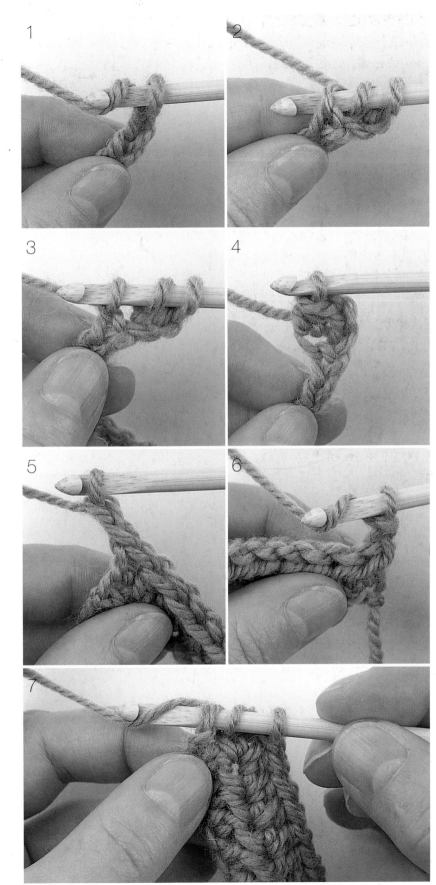

WORKING A DOUBLE CROCHET STITCH

Taller than either of the previous two stitches, double crochet is easy to work and the fabric grows quickly. It has a more open appearance than single crochet and less tendency to curl up at the edges.

1 Wrap the yarn over the hook and insert the hook from front to back into the work. (If you are at the beginning of the row, insert the hook under the top loop of the fourth chain from the hook.) Draw the yarn through the chain, leaving 3 loops on the hook.

2 Wrap the yarn over the hook and draw it through the first 2 loops on the hook. Two loops remain on the hook.

3 Wrap the yarn over the hook. Draw the yarn through the 2 loops on the hook. One loop remains on the hook and 1 double crochet stitch has been worked.

4 At the end of the row, work 3 chains for the turning chain and turn the work.

5 Skipping the first double crochet stitch at the beginning of the row, wrap the yarn over the hook, insert the hook from front to back under both loops of the second stitch on the previous row, and work a double crochet stitch into each stitch made on the previous row.

6 At the end of the row, work the last stitch into the top stitch of the turning chain.

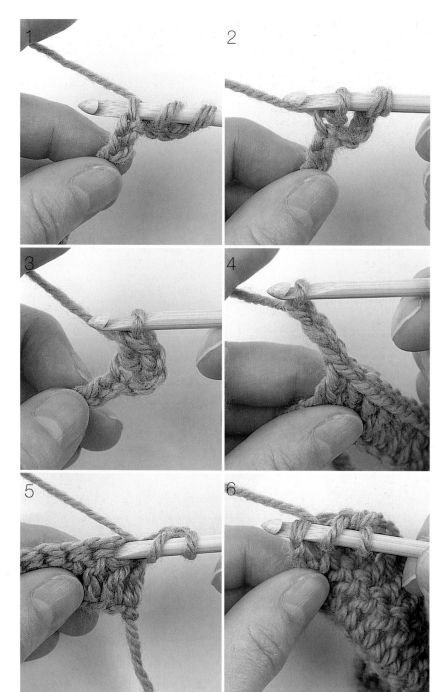

WORKING INTO THE BACK LOOP

Unless specific pattern instructions tell you otherwise, it's usual to work most crochet stitches by taking the hook under both loops of the stitches made on the previous row. By working under the back loop of a stitch, the unworked loop becomes a horizontal bar that creates ridged fabric.

To work into the back of a row of stitches, insert the hook under the back loops of the stitches on the previous row.

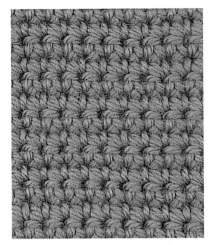

single crochet

half double crochet

double crochet

Working in rounds

Crochet can easily be worked in rounds, beginning at the center and working outward. To make the foundation, work a short length of chain and join it into a ring.

1 Begin making the foundation ring by working a short length of chain (page 12). Work the number of chains stated in the pattern and join into a ring by working a slip stitch (page 14) into the first stitch of the foundation chain. Gently tighten the first stitch by pulling the loose yarn end with your left hand. The foundation ring is now complete.

2 Work the number of starting chains stated in the pattern: 3 chains are shown here and will count as a double crochet stitch.

3 Inserting the hook into the space at the center of the ring each time, work the correct number of stitches into the ring as stated in the pattern. Count the stitches at the end of the round to make sure you have worked the correct number.

4 Join the first and last stitches of the round together by working a slip stitch into the top of the starting chain.

Joining a new yarn

Always join new yarn at the side of the work, not in the middle of a row, to help prevent the yarn ends from unraveling and making a hole in your work. Join the new yarn as you work the last stitch of the row, whether working in single or double crochet.

JOINING A NEW YARN IN SINGLE CROCHET

1 Join the new color at the end of the last row worked in the previous color. To work the last stitch, draw a loop of the old yarn through so there are 2 loops on the hook and loop the new yarn around the hook.

2 Pull the new yarn through both stitches on the hook. Turn and work the next row with the new color.

JOINING A NEW YARN IN DOUBLE CROCHET

1 Join the new color at the end of the last row worked in the previous color. Leaving the last stage of the final stitch incomplete, loop the new yarn around the hook and pull it though the stitches on the hook to complete the stitch.

2 Turn and work the next row with the new color. Knot the 2 loose ends together before cutting off the excess yarn, leaving a tail of about 4 in. (10 cm). Always undo the knot before darning in the yarn ends.

FASTENING OFF YARN

To fasten off the yarn at the end of a piece of crochet, cut the yarn 6 in. (15 cm) from the last stitch and pull the yarn end through the stitch with the hook. (Right.)

DEALING WITH YARN ENDS

Thread the end of the yarn in a yarn needle. Darn the end through several stitches on the wrong side of the work. Trim the remaining yarn. (Far right.)

OVERCAST SEAM

Crochet pieces are easy to join together as the edges are very stable. Use the same yarn for seaming as for your project and take care to fasten off the yarn ends securely.

1 Pin the crochet pieces together with right sides facing, inserting the pins vertically a few stitches away from the edge. Secure the yarn by taking a few stitches over the top of the edge.

2 With your index finger between the layers, insert the needle from back to front through both layers as close to the edge as you can. Repeat evenly along the seam.

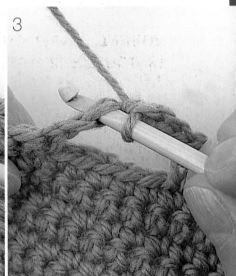

MAKING A BUTTONHOLE

Working a two-row horizontal buttonhole is the neatest method of making any size of buttonhole and has the advantage of not needing any reinforcing. You can make this type of buttonhole on either a right side row as shown, or on a wrong side row.

1 On a right side row, work in single crochet to the position of the buttonhole, skip the number of stitches indicated in the pattern, and work the same number of chains over the skipped stitches.

2 Anchor the chain by working a single crochet stitch after the skipped stitches. Continue along the row working single crochet stitches.

3 On the return (wrong side) row, work a single crochet stitch into each stitch. When you reach the buttonhole, work a single crochet stitch into each chain, then complete the row in single crochet.

Shaping crochet

There are several different ways to shape crochet by increasing or decreasing the number of working stitches. Adding or subtracting one or two stitches at intervals along a row of crochet is the easiest way and the methods shown on this page can be used with single, half double, and double crochet stitches.

INCREASING

1 The simplest method of adding a single stitch to a row of single crochet is by working 2 single crochet stitches into 1 stitch on the previous row.

2 This type of increase is also used when working double crochet. Work 2 double crochet stitches into 1 stitch on the previous row.

WORKING TWO OR THREE STITCHES TOGETHER

1 Decrease 1 single crochet stitch by working 2 stitches together (known as "sc2tog"). Leave the first stitch incomplete so there are 2 loops on the hook.

2 Draw the yarn through the next stitch so there are 3 loops on the hook.

3 To finish the decrease, wrap the yarn over and pull through all 3 loops on the hook.

4 Two stitches can be decreased in the same way by working 3 single crochet stitches together (known as "sc3tog").

DECREASING

To decrease one stitch along a row of crochet, either skip one stitch or work two adjacent stitches together. To decrease two stitches, work three adjacent stitches together to make one stitch. The easiest way to decrease one stitch—whether working in single or double crochet—is by simply skipping the next stitch of the row, as shown below.

Gauge

The term "gauge" refers to the number of stitches and rows contained in a given width and length of crocheted fabric. The patterns in this book include a recommended gauge for the yarn used and it's important that you match this gauge so your work comes out the right size. This is usually quoted as "x stitches and y rows to 4 in. (10 cm)" measured over a certain stitch pattern using a certain size of hook. Gauge can be affected by the type of yarn, the size and brand of the hook, and the type of stitch pattern. For some items, such as scarves and bags, getting the correct gauge is less important than when making mittens or slippers, where a good fit is crucial.

MAKING AND MEASURING A GAUGE SAMPLE

Read the pattern instructions to find the recommended gauge. Working in the exact yarn you will use for the item, make a sample 6–8 in. (15–20 cm) wide. Work in the required stitch until the piece is 6–8 in. (15–20 cm) long. Fasten off the yarn. Block the gauge sample using the method suited to the yarn fiber content and allow to dry.

1 Lay the sample right side up on a flat surface and use a ruler or tape measure to measure 4 in. (10 cm) horizontally across a row of stitches. Mark this measurement by inserting 2 pins exactly 4 in. (10 cm) apart. Make a note of the number of stitches (including partial stitches) between the pins. This is the number of stitches to 4 in. (10 cm).

2 Turn the sample on its side. Working in the same way, measure 4 in. (10 cm) across the rows, again inserting 2 pins exactly 4 in. (10 cm) apart. Make a note of the number of rows (including partial rows) between the pins. This is the number of rows to 4 in. (10 cm).

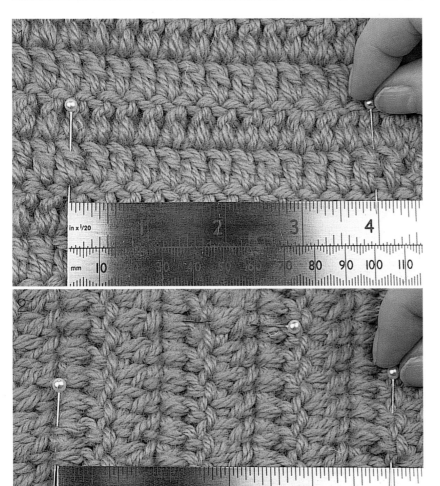

Ball bands

The ball band—or paper tag on yarn—has lots of useful information printed on it, including the fiber content of the yarn, its weight, and the yardage of the ball or skein. Some bands also include suggested crochet hook sizes and gauge measurements, as well as washing or dry-cleaning information.

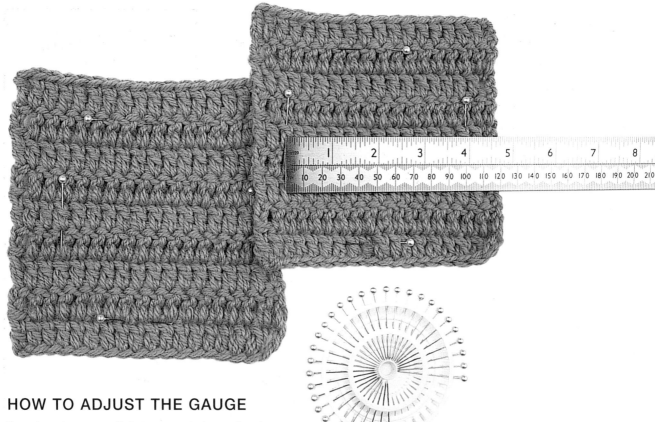

HOW TO ADJUST THE GAUGE

If you have too many stitches or rows between the pins inserted in your gauge sample, your gauge is too tight and you should make another sample using a hook one size larger. If you have too few stitches or rows between the pins, your gauge is too loose and you should make another sample using a hook one size smaller. Block the new sample and measure the gauge as before. Repeat this process until your gauge matches that given in the pattern.

PRESSING CROCHETED FABRIC

Press the fabric lightly on the wrong side, setting your iron temperature according to the information given on the ball band of your yarn. Avoid pressing synthetic yarns as they will become limp and lifeless—or melt—with too much heat.

BLOCKING CROCHETED FABRIC

Blocking involves pinning a piece of crocheted fabric to the correct size, then either steaming it with an iron or moistening with cold water depending on the fiber content of the yarn. Pin your finished item to the correct size on a flat surface, such as an ironing board or a specialist blocking board, using rust-proof pins. It is a good idea to block gauge samples (page 21) before measuring them.

Woolen

(Above) To block woolen yarns with warm steam, hold a steam iron set at the correct temperature for the yarn about $^3/_4$ in. (2 cm) above the surface of the crochet and let the steam penetrate for several seconds without allowing the iron to come into contact with the fabric. Lay the board flat and allow to dry before removing the pins.

Synthetics

(Below) To block synthetic and wool/synthetic blend yarns, pin out as above, then use a spray bottle to mist the item with clean cold water until it is evenly moist all over, but not saturated. Pat with your hand to help the moisture penetrate more easily. Lay the board flat and allow to dry before removing the pins.

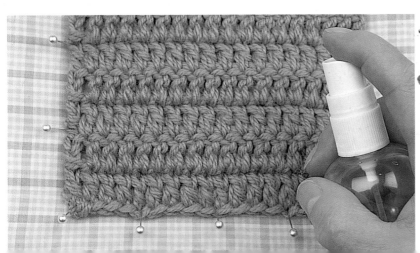

Standard crochet abbreviations
alt – alternate
approx – approximately
beg – beginning
CC – contrast color
ch – refers to chain or space previously made, such as ch-1 space
ch(s) – chain(s)
cont – continue
dc – double crochet
foll – following
hdc – half double crochet
MC – main color
patt – pattern
rem – remaining
rep – repeat
RS – right side
sc – single crochet
sc2tog – single crochet two stitches together
sc3tog – single crochet three stitches together
sk – skip
sl st – slip stitch
sp(s) – space(s)
st(s) – stitch(es)
WS – wrong side

Basic Patterns

This section of the book contains basic patterns for a crocheted scarf, buttonhole bag, hat, and pairs of slippers and mittens. If you're a beginner, start by making the basic scarf on this page, then try the hat on page 26.

THE BASIC SCARF

YOU WILL NEED

- 2 balls of pure wool chunky yarn with approx 100 yds (92 m) per 100 g ball
- Size J (6 mm) and size K (6.5 mm) crochet hooks or sizes needed to achieve gauge
- Yarn needle

FINISHED SIZE

Scarf measures 6 in. (15 cm) wide and 40 in. (102 cm) long.

GAUGE

12 stitches and 6 rows to 4 in. (10 cm) measured over double crochet, using size J (6 mm) crochet hook.

CROCHETING THE SCARF

Using size K (6.5 mm) hook, ch 22.

Change to size J (6 mm) hook.

ROW 1: (RS) 1 dc into 4th ch from hook, 1 dc into each ch to end, turn.

ROW 2: Ch 3 (counts as 1 dc), 1 dc into each dc of previous row, working last dc into 3rd of beg skipped ch 3, turn.

ROW 3: Ch 3 (counts as 1 dc), 1 dc into each dc of previous row, working last dc into 3rd of ch 3, turn. (20 sc)

Rep Row 3 until scarf measures 40 in. (102 cm) long, ending with a RS row.

Fasten off yarn.

FINISHING THE SCARF

Press lightly on the wrong side (Pressing, page 22). Darn the yarn ends on the wrong side using the yarn needle (Dealing With Yarn Ends, page 18).

YOU WILL NEED

- 2 balls of pure wool chunky yarn with approx 100 yds (92 m) per 100 g ball
- Size J (6 mm) and size K (6.5 mm) crochet hooks or sizes needed to achieve gauge
- Yarn needle

FINISHED SIZE

Bag measures 9½ in. (24 cm) deep and 11 in. (28 cm) wide.

GAUGE

14 stitches and 16 rows to 4 in. (10 cm) measured over single crochet, using size J (6 mm) crochet hook.

CROCHETING THE BAG FRONT

Using size K (6.5 mm) hook, ch 33.

Change to size J (6 mm) hook.

ROW 1: (RS) 1 sc into 2nd ch from hook, 1 sc into each ch to end, turn.

ROW 2: Ch 1, 1 sc into each sc of previous row, turn. (32 sc)

Rep Row 2 twenty-seven times more, ending with a RS row.

Make buttonhole

ROW 1: (WS) Ch 1, 1 sc into each of next 10 sc, ch 12, sk next 12 sc, 1 sc into each of next 10 sc, turn.

ROW 2: Ch 1, 1 sc into each of next 10 sc, 1 sc into each of next 12 chs, 1 sc into each of next 10 sc, turn. (32 sc)

Make handle

ROW 1: Ch 1, 1 sc into each sc of previous row, turn.

Rep Row 1 three times more, ending with a RS row.

Fasten off yarn.

CROCHETING THE BAG BACK

Work as for front.

FINISHING THE BAG

Press the pieces lightly on the wrong side (Pressing, page 22). Darn the yarn ends on the wrong side using the yarn needle (Dealing With Yarn Ends, page 18). Place the pieces together with right sides facing and pin around the edges. Using the same yarn in the yarn needle, join side and base seams. Turn bag to right side.

THE BASIC HAT

YOU WILL NEED

- 1 ball of pure wool chunky yarn with approx 100 yds (92 m) per 100 g ball
- Crochet hook size J (6 mm) or size needed to achieve gauge
- Yarn needle

FINISHED SIZE

Hat measures 8 in. (20 cm) deep and 22 in. (56 cm) in circumference and will fit average adult head.

GAUGE

12 stitches and $6\frac{1}{2}$ rows to 4 in. (10 cm) measured over double crochet worked with size J (6 mm) hook.

MAKING THE HAT

FOUNDATION RING: Ch 6 and join with sl st to form a ring.

ROUND 1: Ch 3 (counts as 1 dc), 15 dc into ring, join with sl st into 3rd of ch 3. (16 dc)

ROUND 2. Ch 3 (counts as 1 dc), 1 dc into same stitch, 2 dc into each rem dc of previous round, join with sl st into 3rd of ch 3. (32 dc)

ROUND 3: Ch 3 (counts as 1 dc), 1 dc into same stitch, * 1 dc into each of next 3 dc, 2 dc into next dc; rep from * to last 3 dc, 1 dc into each of next 3 dc, join with sl st into 3rd of ch 3. (40 dc)

ROUND 4: Ch 3 (counts as 1 dc), 1 dc into same stitch, * 1 dc into each of next 4 dc, 2 dc into next dc; rep from * to last 4 dc, 1 dc into each of next 4 dc, join with sl st into 3rd of ch 3. (48 dc)

ROUND 5: Ch 3 (counts as 1 dc), 1 dc into same stitch, * 1 dc into each of next 5 dc, 2 dc into next dc; rep from * to last 5 dc, 1 dc into each of next 5 dc, join with sl st into 3rd of ch 3. (56 dc)

ROUND 6: Ch 3 (counts as 1 dc), 1 dc into same stitch, * 1 dc into each of next 6 dc, 2 dc into next dc; rep from * to last 6 dc, 1 dc into each of next 6 dc, join with sl st into 3rd of ch 3. (64 dc)

ROUNDS 7–10: Ch 3 (counts as 1 dc), sk first dc, 1 dc into each rem dc of previous round, join with sl st into 3rd of ch 3.

ROUND 11: Ch 1, 1 sc into same stitch, 1 sc into each rem dc of previous round, join with sl st into first sc.

ROUNDS 12–14: Ch 1, 1 sc into same stitch, 1 sc into each rem sc of previous round, join with sl st into first sc.
Fasten off yarn.

FINISHING THE HAT

Press lightly on the wrong side (Pressing, page 22). Darn the yarn ends on the wrong side using the yarn needle (Dealing With Yarn Ends, page 18).

THE BASIC SLIPPERS

YOU WILL NEED

- 2 [2, 3] balls of pure wool Icelandic Lopi yarn with approx 109 yds (100 m) per 100 g ball
- Crochet hooks size J (6 mm) and size K (6.5 mm) or sizes needed to achieve gauge
- Yarn needle

FINISHED SIZE

To fit sizes Small (to fit up to 9 in./23 cm sole), Medium (to fit up to 10 in./25.5 cm sole) and Large (to fit up to 11 in./28 cm sole). Instructions for Medium and Large sizes are given in square brackets.

GAUGE

14 stitches and 16 rows to 4 in. (10 cm) measured over single crochet worked with size J (6 mm) hook.

MAKING THE SLIPPERS (make two)

FOUNDATION CHAIN: Using size K (6.5 mm) hook, ch 21 [25, 29].

Change to size J (6 mm) hook.

ROUND 1: (RS) 2 sc into 2nd ch from hook, 1 sc into each of next 9 [11, 13] chs, 1 hdc into next ch, 1 dc into each of next 7 [9, 11] chs, 2 dc into next ch, 5 dc into last ch; working along opposite side of chain, 2 dc into next ch, 1 dc into each of next 7 [9, 11] chs, 1 hdc into next ch, 1 sc into each of next 9 [11, 13] chs, 2 sc into last ch, join with sl st into first sc. (47 [55, 63] sts)

ROUND 2: Ch 1, 1 sc into first st, 2 sc into next st, 1 sc into each of next 12 [14, 16] sts, 1 hdc into each of next 8 [10, 12] sts, 2 hdc into next st, 3 hdc into next st, 2 hdc into next st, 1 hdc into each of next 8 [10, 12] sts, 1 sc into each of next 13 [15, 17] sts, 2 sc into last st, join with sl st into first sc. (53 [61, 69] sts)

ROUND 3: Ch 1, 1 sc into first st, 2 sc into next st, 1 sc into each of next 10 [12, 14] sts, sk next st, 1 sc into each of next 11 [13, 15] sts, 2 sc into next st, 1 sc into each of next 5 sts, 2 sc into next st, 1 sc into each of next 11 [13, 15] sts, sk next st, 1 sc into each of next 9 [11, 13] sts, 2 sc into last st, join with sl st into first sc. (55 [63, 71] sts)

ROUNDS 4, 5, and 6: Ch 1, 1 sc into each st of previous round, join with sl st into first sc.

ROUND 7: Ch 1, 1 sc into each of next 20 [24, 28] sts, [sc2tog, 1 sc into next st] three times, [1 sc into next st, sc2tog] three times, 1 sc into each of next 17 [21, 25] sts, join with sl st into first sc. (49 [57, 65] sts)

ROUND 8: Ch 1, 1 sc into each of next 20 [24, 28] sts, sc2tog six times, 1 sc into each of next 17 [21, 25] sts, join with sl st into first sc. (43 [51, 59] sts)

ROUND 9: Ch 1, 1 sc into each of next 20 [24, 28] sts, sc2tog three times, 1 sc into each of next 17 [21, 25] sts, join with sl st into first sc. (40 [48, 56] sts)

ROUND 10: Ch 1, 1 sc into each st of previous round, join with sl st into first sc.

ROUND 11: Ch 1, 1 sc into each of next 22 [26, 30] sts, sk next st, 1 sc into each of next 17 [21, 25] sts, join with sl st into first sc. (39 [47, 55] sts)

ROUND 12: Ch 1, 1 sc into each of next 20 [24, 28] sts, sc3tog, 1 sc into each of next 16 [20, 24] sts, join with sl st into first sc. (37 [45, 53] sts)

ROUND 13: Sl st into each st worked on previous round, join with sl st into first sl st.

Fasten off yarn.

FINISHING THE SLIPPERS

Press lightly on the wrong side (Pressing, page 22). Darn the yarn ends on the wrong side using the yarn needle (Dealing With Yarn Ends, page 18).

THE BASIC MITTENS

YOU WILL NEED

- 2 [2, 2] balls of pure wool chunky yarn with approx 100 yds (92 m) per 100 g ball
- Crochet hooks size H (5.5 mm) and size J (6 mm) or sizes needed to achieve gaug
- Yarn needle
- Split ring marker

FINISHED SIZE

To fit sizes Small (to fit up to 8 in./20 cm around hand), Medium (to fit up to 9 in./23 cm around hand), and Large (to fit up to 10 in./25.5 cm around hand). Instructions for Medium and Large sizes are given in square brackets.

GAUGE

14 stitches and 16 rows to 4 in. (10 cm) measured over single crochet worked with size J (6 mm) hook.

MAKING THE RIGHT MITTEN

Make cuff

** FOUNDATION CHAIN: Using size J (6 mm) hook, ch 6 [8, 10].

Change to size H (5.5 mm) hook.

FOUNDATION ROW: 1 sc into 2nd ch from hook, 1 sc into each ch to end, turn. (5 [7, 9] sts)

ROW 1: Ch 1, working into back loops only, 1 sc into first sc, 1 sc into each sc to end, turn.

Rep Row 1 20 [22, 24] times more, ending with a WS row.

Work body

Change to size J (6 mm) hook.

ROW 1: Ch 1, working into row ends along side edge of cuff, 2 sc into first row end, 1 sc into each rem row end, turn. (23 [25, 27] sts)

ROW 2: Ch 1, 1 sc into each sc to end, turn.

Rep Row 2 zero [2, 4] times more, ending with a WS row. ******

Shape thumb gusset

ROW 1: Ch 1, 1 sc into each of next 13 [14, 15] sc, 2 sc into next sc, 1 sc into next sc, 2 sc into next sc, 1 sc into each of next 7 [8, 9] sc, turn. (25 [27, 29] sts)

ROW 2: Ch 1, 1 sc into each of next 7 [8, 9] sc, 2 sc into next sc, 1 sc into each of next 3 sc, 2 sc into next sc, 1 sc into each of next 13 [14, 15] sc, turn. (27 [29, 31] sts)

ROW 3: Ch 1, 1 sc into each of next 13 [14, 15] sc, 2 sc into next sc, 1 sc into each of next 5 sc, 2 sc into next sc, 1 sc into each of next 7 [8, 9] sc, turn. (29 [31, 33] sts)

ROW 4: Ch 1, 1 sc into each of next 7 [8, 9] sc, 2 sc into next sc, 1 sc into each of next 7 sc, 2 sc into next sc, 1 sc into each of next 13 [14, 15] sc, turn. (31 [33, 35] sts)

ROW 5: Ch 1, 1 sc into each of next 13 [14, 15] sc, 2 sc into next sc, 1 sc into each of next 9 sc, 2 sc into next sc, 1 sc into each of next 7 [8, 9] sc, turn. (33 [35, 37] sts)

ROW 6: Ch 1, 1 sc into each of next 8 [9, 10] sc, ch 1 (place marker in ch), sk next 11 sc, 1 sc into each of next 14 [15, 16] sc, turn.

ROW 7: Ch 1, 1 sc into each sc and ch-1 sp to end of row, turn. (23 [25, 27] sts)

Work even in sc for 9 [11, 13] more rows, ending with a WS row.

Shape top

*** ROW 1: Ch 1, sc2tog, 1 sc into each of next 7 [8, 9] sc, sc2tog, 1 sc into next sc, sc2tog, 1 sc into each of next 7 [8, 9] sc, sc2tog, turn. (19 [21, 23] sts)

ROW 2: Ch 1, 1 sc into each sc, turn.

ROW 3: Ch 1, sc2tog, 1 sc into each of next 5 [6, 7] sc, sc2tog, 1 sc into next sc, sc2tog, 1 sc into each of next 5 [6, 7] sc, sc2tog, turn. (15 [17, 19] sts)

ROW 4: Rep Row 2.

ROW 5: Ch 1, sc2tog, 1 sc into each of next 3 [4, 5] sc, sc2tog, 1 sc into next sc, sc2tog, 1 sc into each of next 3 [4, 5] sc, sc2tog, turn. (11 [13, 15] sts).

Fasten off yarn.

Work thumb

With RS of work facing and size J (6 mm) hook, rejoin yarn with sl st to marked ch.

ROUND 1: Ch 1, 1 sc into same sp as sl st, 1 sc into each sc; join with sl st to first sc. (12 [12, 12] sts)

Rep Round 1 six [8, 10] times more.

NEXT ROUND: Ch 1, sc2tog six times. (6 [6, 6] sts)

Fasten off yarn leaving 8 in. (20 cm) tail. Thread tail in yarn needle, draw through rem sts and fasten off tightly.***

MAKING THE LEFT MITTEN

Work as given for right mitten from ** to **.

Shape thumb gusset

ROW 1: Ch 1, 1 sc into each of next 7 [8, 9] sc, 2 sc into next sc, 1 sc into next sc, 2 sc into next sc, 1 sc into each of next 13 [14, 15] sc, turn. (25 [27, 29] sts)

ROW 2: Ch 1, 1 sc into each of next 13 [14, 15] sc, 2 sc into next sc, 1 sc into each of next 3 sc, 2 sc into next sc, 1 sc into each of next 7 [8, 9] sc, turn. (27 [29, 31] sts)

ROW 3: Ch 1, 1 sc into each of next 7 [8, 9] sc, 2 sc into next sc, 1 sc into each of next 5 sc, 2 sc into next sc, 1 sc into each of next 13 [14, 15] sc, turn. (29 [31, 33] sts)

ROW 4: Ch 1, 1 sc into each of next 13 [14, 15] sc, 2 sc into next sc, 1 sc into each of next 7 sc, 2 sc into next sc, 1 sc into each of next 7 [8, 9] sc, turn. (31 [33, 35] sts)

ROW 5: Ch 1, 1 sc into each of next 7 [8, 9] sc, 2 sc into next sc, 1 sc into each of next 9 sc, 2 sc into next sc, 1 sc into each of next 13 [14, 15] sc, turn. (33 [35, 37] sts)

ROW 6: Ch 1, 1 sc into each of next 15 [16, 17] sc, ch 1 (place marker in ch), sk next 11 sc, 1 sc into each of next 7 [8, 9] sc, turn.

ROW 7: Ch 1, 1 sc into each sc and ch-1 sp to end of row, turn. (23 [25, 27] sts)

Work even in sc for 9 [11, 13] more rows, ending with a WS row.

Work as given for right mitten from *** to ***.

FINISHING THE MITTENS

Press the mittens lightly on the wrong side (Pressing, page 22).

Darn the yarn ends on the wrong side using the yarn needle (Dealing With Yarn Ends, page 18). With right sides together and matching yarn in the yarn needle, join the top and side seams.

chapter 2
edgings and
and trimmings

From **pom-poms** and **fringes** to **tassels** and **flower trims**, Chapter 2 covers a wide range of easy-to-apply edgings and decorations. The humble granny square is brought up-to-date and put into service as a funky pocket on Jazz, a hot pink scarf. Gloriously **ruffled cuffs** turn a pair of plain mittens into a flirty, girly creation called Florence. Crochet edgings feature in this chapter, from the pretty **shell edging** on Priscilla to the smart and stylish edging on College.

susie

narrow scarf with pom-poms

An edging of shaggy pom-poms makes a narrow scarf into a fun accessory. Add one pom-pom to each corner and space the others at regular intervals along the edges, leaving a short length of yarn between pom-pom and crochet so the pom-poms hang down gracefully.

YOU WILL NEED

- 2 balls of pure wool DK yarn with approx 137 yds (125 m) per 50 g ball in main color
- 3 balls of the same yarn in contrasting color
- Size J (6 mm) and size K (6.5 mm) crochet hooks or sizes needed to achieve gauge
- Yarn needle

FINISHED SIZE

Scarf measures $2^3/4$ in. (7 cm) wide and 45 in. (114 cm) long.

GAUGE

12 stitches and 6 rows to 4 in. (10 cm) measured over double crochet using size J (6 mm) hook and two strands of main yarn held together.

WORKING THE SCARF

Crochet and finish the scarf following the basic pattern on page 24, but begin with a foundation chain of 11 instead of 22. Work in double crochet until the scarf measures 45 in. (114 cm) long.

MAKING AND APPLYING THE POM-POMS

1 Using 2 strands of contrasting yarn held together, wind yarn between fixed points (see Tip) to make a hank of approximately 100 strands.

2 Cut 55 in. (140 cm) lengths of main yarn (you'll need 22 lengths, 1 for tying each pom-pom). Fold a length of cut yarn in half and tie it around center of hank in a square knot.

3 Fold yarn ends around hank and knot once again to secure. Repeat at 3 in. (8 cm) intervals along hank.

4 Remove tied hank from fixed points and lay flat. Cut through hank between yarn ties with sharp scissors. Take care not to cut through ties by mistake. Repeat Steps 1–4 until you have made 22 pom-poms.

5 Fluff out ends of pom-poms, trimming off any straggly yarn ends. Use ties threaded in yarn needle to attach a pom-pom to each corner of scarf, leaving about 1 in. (2.5 cm) of tie between pom-pom and scarf. Attach 9 pom-poms to each long edge of scarf, spacing them evenly along edge, and adding 1 to each corner.

Tip

The scarf is worked with two strands of DK yarn in main color held together throughout. When winding the yarn to make the pom-poms, you need two fixed points approximately 30 in. (76 cm) apart, such as two cupboard door knobs or two quick-release clamps fixed to a table.

priscilla

scarf with shell edging

A row of simple shell edging makes a pretty, contrasting trim at each end of a scarf. Work a few rows of single crochet into the edge first, to make a firm foundation for the shells, using the same weight of yarn as the scarf.

YOU WILL NEED

- 2 balls of pure wool chunky yarn in main color with approx 100 yds (92 m) per 100 g ball
- Leftovers of the same yarn in contrasting color
- Size I (5.5 mm), size J (6 mm), and size K (6.5 mm) crochet hooks or sizes needed to achieve gauge
- Yarn needle

FINISHED SIZE

Scarf measures 6 in. (15 cm) wide and 40 in. (102 cm) long, not including edging.

GAUGE

12 stitches and 6 rows to 4 in. (10 cm) over double crochet using size J (6 mm) hook or size needed to achieve gauge.

WORKING THE SCARF

Crochet and finish the scarf following the basic pattern on page 24.

Prefer the slippers? see page 27 for the basic pattern

WORKING THE EDGING

1 Using size I (5.5 mm) hook, join contrasting yarn to right side of scarf end. Chain 1, then work 2 single crochet into first stitch. Continue along row, working 1 single crochet into each stitch along end of scarf. (21 sc)

2 Turn at end of row, chain 1 and work 1 single crochet into each stitch of previous row.

3 Turn, chain 1 and work 1 single crochet into first stitch. *Skip next 2 stitches and work 5 double crochet into next stitch to make a shell.

4 Finish shell by skipping next 2 stitches and working 1 single crochet into next stitch. Repeat from * to end of row. Fasten off yarn and darn in ends.

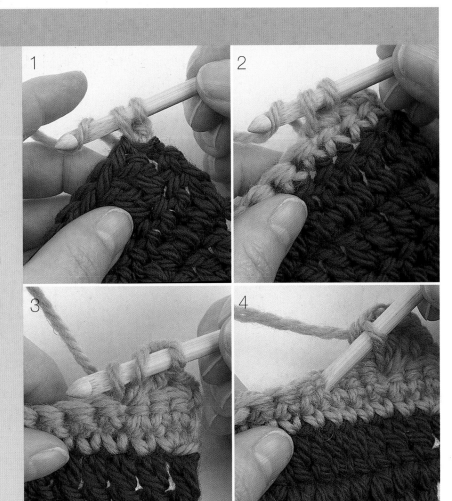

shell-edged slippers

Shell edging works well around the top of slippers. Omit the row of slip stitches in the basic pattern and work the edging directly into the top of the slippers using a contrasting yarn color.

jazz

scarf with granny square pockets

Brighten up a plain scarf by adding a granny square pocket to each end. Work the pockets in the main yarn plus a contrasting yarn or work each round in a different color for extra effect.

YOU WILL NEED

- 2 balls of pure wool chunky yarn in main color (MC) with approx 100 yds (92 m) per 100 g ball
- Leftovers of the same yarn in a contrasting color (CC)
- Size J (6 mm) and size K (6.5 mm) crochet hooks or sizes needed to achieve gauge
- Yarn needle

FINISHED SIZE

Scarf measures 6 in. (15 cm) wide and 40 in. (102 cm) long. Pocket measures 6 in. (15 cm) square.

GAUGE

12 stitches and 6 rows to 4 in. (10 cm) measured over double crochet using size J (6 mm) hook, or size needed to achieve gauge.

WORKING THE SCARF

Crochet and finish the scarf following the basic pattern on page 24.

Working the pockets (make two)

YARN: Worked in two colors, MC and CC.

FOUNDATION RING: Using CC, ch 6 and join with sl st to form a ring.

ROUND 1: Ch 3 (counts as 1 dc), 2 dc into ring, ch 3, *3 dc into ring, ch 3; rep from * twice more, join with sl st into 3rd of ch-3. Break off CC.

ROUND 2: Join MC to any ch-3 sp, ch 3 (counts as 1 dc), [2 dc, ch 3, 3 dc] into same sp (corner made), *ch 1, [3 dc, ch 3, 3 dc] into next ch-3 sp; rep from * twice more, ch 1, join with sl st into 3rd of ch-3. Break off MC.

ROUND 3: Join CC to any ch-3 corner sp, ch 3 (counts as 1 dc), [2 dc, ch 3, 3 dc] into same sp, *ch 1, 3 dc into ch-1

sp, ch 1, **[3 dc, ch 3, 3 dc] into next ch-3 corner sp; rep from * twice and from * to ** once again, join with sl st into 3rd of ch-3. Break off CC.

ROUND 4: Join MC to any ch-3 corner sp, ch 3 (counts as 1 dc), [2 dc, ch 3, 3 dc] into same sp, *[ch 1, 3 dc] into each ch-1 sp along side of square, ch 1, **[3 dc, ch 3, 3 dc] into next ch-3 corner sp; rep from * twice and from * to ** once again, join with sl st into 3rd of ch-3.

ROUND 5: Ch 1, 1 sc into same place as sl st, 1 sc into each dc on previous round, working 3 sc into each ch-3 sp and 1 sc into each ch-1 sp, join with sl st into first sc.

Fasten off yarn and darn in all ends.

Prefer the bag? see page 25 for the basic pattern

MAKING THE POCKETS

1 Using contrasting yarn, work foundation ring and Round 1. Join round by working a slip stitch through third of 3 starting chains and fasten off yarn.

2 Join main yarn to any chain space worked on Round 1 by placing a slip knot on hook, inserting it into chain space and working a slip stitch to secure new yarn.

3 Work corners on Rounds 2, 3, and 4 by working a group of 3 double crochet stitches separated by 3 chains into each corner space worked on previous round.

4 On final round, work 1 single crochet stitch into each stitch made on previous round. As you proceed around square, work 3 single crochet stitches into each corner space and 1 single crochet stitch into each of smaller spaces along sides.

5 Pin 1 finished square to each end of scarf. Join 3 sides of each square onto scarf with overcast seam to make pockets, working stitches through outer loops of final row of stitches around squares.

pocket bag

A granny square makes an unusual yet practical pocket for a buttonhole bag. Pin the pocket in place and use matching yarn to backstitch the sides and lower edge of the square to the bag, taking each stitch through both loops of the final round of the square.

summer

bag with crochet flower trim

Stitching chunky crochet flowers onto a cream buttonhole bag is a quick way to add a summery look to a plain crocheted surface. Choose bright yarn colors to make the flowers and stitch each one securely in place using the yarn tail.

YOU WILL NEED

- 4 balls of pure wool DK yarn with approx 137 yds (125 m) per 50 g ball in main color
- Leftovers of chunky yarn in 3 contrasting colors
- Size I (5.5 mm), size J (6 mm), and size K (6.5 mm) crochet hooks or sizes needed to achieve gauge
- Yarn needle

FINISHED SIZE

Bag measures 9¹/₂ in. (24 cm) deep, including handles, and 11 in. (28 cm) wide. Flowers are approximately 3 in. (8 cm) in diameter.

GAUGE

14 stitches and 16 rows to 4 in. (10 cm) measured over single crochet using size J (6 mm) hook and two strands of main yarn held together.

NOTE

The bag is worked with two strands of DK yarn held together throughout; the flowers are worked with one strand of chunky yarn.

WORKING THE BAG

Crochet the bag front and back pieces following the basic pattern on page 25.

WORKING THE FLOWERS
(make four)

YARN: Worked in 3 contrasting colors.

FOUNDATION RING: Using first color and size I (5.5 mm) hook, ch 6 and join with sl st to form a ring.

ROUND 1: Ch 3 (counts as 1 dc), 14 dc into ring, join with sl st into 3rd of ch-3. Break off first color.

ROUND 2: Join second color to any dc, 1 sc into same st, *3 dc into each of next 2 dc, 1 sc into next dc; rep from * to last 2 sts, 3 dc into each of last 2 dc, join with sl st into first sc.

Fasten off yarn, leaving a long tail. Darn in all other yarn ends except for the long tail. Make 2 flowers using the same color combination and 2 flowers using first color at the center and third color for the petals.

WORKING THE FLOWERS

1 Using first color, work foundation ring and Round 1. Join the round by working a slip stitch through third of 3 starting chains and fasten off yarn. Join second color to any stitch worked on Round 1 by inserting hook into stitch and pulling loop of new yarn through it.

2 With new yarn, work 1 slip stitch then 1 single crochet into same stitch.

3 Work 3 double crochet into each of next 2 stitches to make first petal.

4 Work 3 more petals around motif, leaving 2 stitches remaining. Work 3 double crochet into each of these stitches, then join the round by working 1 slip stitch into first single crochet of round.

5 Using photograph as guide, pin finished flowers to front of bag. Using yarn tails, stitch each flower to bag, taking 2 or 3 small stitches between each petal, and stitching through both flower and bag. Secure yarn neatly on wrong side.

FINISHING THE BAG

Finish the bag as given in the basic pattern on page 25.

arizona

bag with yarn fringe

A simple fringe makes a great finishing touch along the bottom edge of a bag. You can use the same yarn as the bag or give it a different look by making the fringe in another color or texture of yarn. Making a fringe is a great opportunity to use up leftover yarn from your stash.

YOU WILL NEED

- 2 balls of pure wool chunky yarn with approx 100 yds (92 m) per 100 g ball
- Size J (6 mm) and size K (6.5 mm) crochet hooks or sizes needed to achieve gauge
- Yarn needle
- Piece of stiff cardboard

FINISHED SIZE

Bag measures $9\frac{1}{2}$ in. (24 cm) deep, not including fringe, and 11 in. (28 cm) wide.

GAUGE

14 stitches and 16 rows to 4 in. (10 cm) measured over single crochet using size J (6 mm) hook or size needed to achieve gauge.

WORKING THE BAG

Crochet and finish the bag following the basic pattern on page 25.

MAKING THE FRINGE

1 Decide how deep finished fringe will be and cut a rectangle of cardboard to same depth plus 1 in. (2.5 cm). Wind yarn evenly around cardboard and cut along bottom edge to make strands.

2 Insert larger crochet hook from back to front of lower edge of bag. Gather 3 strands into a group, fold in half and loop fold over hook.

3 Carefully pull hook and folded yarn through to wrong side of bag to make loop.

4 Loop hook around cut ends of yarn group and pull gently through to complete tassel. Repeat at regularly spaced intervals along bag edge. Neaten by trimming any long strands.

Prefer the scarf? **see page 24 for the basic pattern**

fringed scarf

A classic fringe finishes off the ends of
a scarf nicely. You can make the fringe
any length you like, but for best results
be generous with the number of
strands you use in each group.

fluffy

shortie mittens with marabou trim

Short, wrist-skimming mittens look great with a fancy edging. It's easy to stitch lengths of brightly colored marabou trim around the cuff, but don't forget to remove it before washing the mittens.

YOU WILL NEED

- 2 [2, 2] balls of pure wool chunky yarn with approx 100 yds (92 m) per 100 g ball
- Size J (6 mm) and size K (6.5 mm) crochet hooks or sizes needed to achieve gauge
- Yarn needle
- Split ring marker
- Sewing thread to match yarn color
- Narrow marabou trim in a contrasting color, approx 10 [11$\frac{1}{2}$, 13] in. (25 [29, 33] cm) for each mitten
- Sewing needle

FINISHED SIZES

To fit sizes Small (to fit up to 8 in./20 cm around hand), Medium (to fit up to 9 in./23 cm around hand), and Large (to fit up to 10 in./25.5 cm around hand). Instructions for Medium and Large sizes are given in square brackets.

GAUGE

14 stitches and 16 rows to 4 in. (10 cm) measured over single crochet using size J (6 mm) hook or size needed to achieve gauge.

Prefer the bag? **see page 25 for the basic pattern**

WORKING THE MITTENS

Using size K (6.5 mm) hook, ch 24 [26, 27]. Change to size J (6 mm) hook.

ROW 1: 1 sc into 2nd ch from hook, 1 sc into each ch to end, turn. (23 [25, 26] sts)

ROW 2: Ch 1, 1 sc into each sc to end, turn.

Rep Row 2 another 2 [2, 4] times, ending with a WS row.

Change to following the basic pattern on pages 28–29, working from "Shape thumb gusset" to end.

Finish mittens as given in basic pattern.

glamorous bag

Marabou trim adds a touch of femininity to a plain pink bag with grab handles. Choose a strongly contrasting color for the trim and position it along the top edge as shown or stitch it around the other three sides as well for a bolder effect.

APPLYING MARABOU TRIM

1 Pin marabou trim around right side of cuff edge of mitten, starting at seam and inserting pins at right angles to edge of crochet.

2 When trim is pinned all the way around, overlap ends of trim by about ³⁄₄ in. (2 cm) and cut off surplus.

3 Working from inside of mitten, stitch trim down by sewing core of it carefully to right side of crochet using sewing thread that matches yarn color. Take stitches through trim at right angles to core, taking care to pull any caught feathers free when making each stitch.

4 Take care when sewing section of trim that overlaps, making sure you catch both ends of trim in with stitches. Secure thread ends neatly on wrong side.

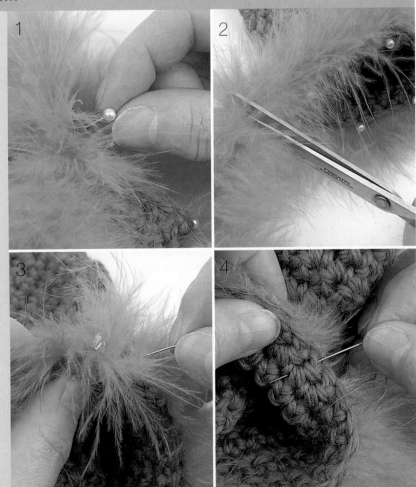

florence

mittens with ruffled cuff

Make a pair of shortie mittens without cuffs and edge them with delicately fluted ruffles. Use two strands of yarn for the mittens and one matching strand for the ruffles, or make the mittens in chunky yarn with contrasting ruffles in thinner yarn.

YOU WILL NEED

- 3 balls of pure wool DK yarn with approx 137 yds (125 m) per 100 g ball
- Size F (4 mm), size J (6 mm), and size K (6.5 mm) crochet hooks or sizes needed to achieve gauge
- Yarn needle

FINISHED SIZE

To fit sizes Small (to fit up to 8 in./20 cm around hand), Medium (to fit up to 9 in./23 cm around hand), and Large (to fit up to 10 in./25.5 cm around hand). Instructions for Medium and Large sizes are given in square brackets. Ruffle measures 1$\frac{1}{2}$ in. (4 cm) deep for all sizes.

GAUGE

14 stitches and 16 rows to 4 in. (10 cm) measured over single crochet using size J (6 mm) hook and two strands of yarn held together.

NOTE

The mittens are worked with two strands of yarn held together throughout; the ruffles are worked with one strand of yarn.

WORKING THE MITTENS

FOUNDATION CHAIN: Using size K (6.5 mm) hook, ch 24 [26, 28]. Change to size J (6 mm) hook.

FOUNDATION ROW: (RS) 1 sc into 2nd ch from hook, 1 sc into each ch to end, turn. (23 [25, 27] sc)

ROW 1: Ch 1, 1 sc into each sc of previous row, turn.

Rep Row 1 another 3 [5, 7] more times, ending with a WS row.

Finish working the mittens by following the basic pattern on pages 28–29 from "Shape thumb gusset," making sure you work one right and one left mitten.

MAKE RUFFLE

With RS of mitten facing, join yarn to cuff edge with one strand of yarn and size F (4 mm) hook.

ROW 1: Ch 3 (counts as 1 dc), 2 dc into first st, 3 dc into each st to end, turn. (69 [75, 81] dc)

ROW 2: Ch 3, 1 dc into each dc of previous row, turn.

ROW 3: Ch 3 (counts as 1 dc), 1 dc into first st, 2 dc into each dc of previous row. (138 [150, 162] dc)

Fasten off yarn.

Prefer the scarf? **see page 24 for the basic pattern**

MAKING THE RUFFLE

1 Make a slip knot in 1 strand of yarn and put it on size F (4 mm) hook. With right side of mitten facing and cuff edge uppermost, insert hook into edge, wrap yarn over hook and make a slip stitch to join yarn.

2 Beginning with turning chain and 2 double crochet stitches worked into first stitch, work 3 double crochet stitches into each stitch along mitten edge and turn.

3 On next row, begin with turning chain and work 1 double crochet stitch into each stitch of previous row and turn.

4 On final row, begin with turning chain and 1 double crochet stitch worked into first stitch. Work 2 double crochet stitches into each remaining stitch of previous row.

FINISHING THE MITTENS

Finish the mittens as given in the basic pattern on pages 28–29.

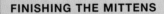

ruffled scarf

Make a narrow scarf in two strands of yarn, beginning with eleven chains and working in double crochet. Using one strand of yarn, work three single crochet stitches into each row end down the long sides of the scarf, then work the ruffle as above. Finish off the edge of each ruffle with a row of single crochet worked in a contrasting color.

college

hat with crab stitch edging

Crab stitch edging makes a firm, corded edge for a plain hat. Unlike most other crochet techniques, the edging is worked from left to right along the round or row.

WORKING THE EDGING

1 Make a slip knot in contrasting yarn and put it on size I (5.5 mm) hook. Insert hook into hat edge close to where rounds join. Wrap yarn over hook and make a slip stitch to join yarn, then work 1 chain.

2 Working from left to right with yarn at back of work, insert hook from front to back into next stitch on right.

3 Wrap yarn over hook and draw loop through from back to front so there are now 2 loops on hook.

4 Wrap yarn over hook, then draw yarn through both loops to complete stitch.

5 Continue to work from left to right, repeating Steps 1, 2, and 3 around edge of hat and joining round with a slip stitch into first stitch.

YOU WILL NEED

- 1 ball of pure wool chunky yarn in main color (MC) with approx 100 yds (92 m) per 100 g ball
- Small amount of the same yarn in contrasting color (CC)
- Size I (5.5 mm), size J (6 mm), and size K (6.5 mm) crochet hooks or sizes needed to achieve gauge
- Yarn needle

FINISHED SIZE

Hat measures 8 in. (20 cm) deep, not including edging, and 22 in. (56 cm) in circumference and will fit average adult head.

GAUGE

12 stitches and 6$\frac{1}{2}$ rows to 4 in. (10 cm) measured over double crochet using size J (6 mm) hook.

MAKING THE HAT

Crochet and finish the hat following the basic pattern on page 26.

Prefer the slippers? see page 27 for the basic pattern

edged slippers

Make a pair of slippers using a solid color of yarn, omitting the last round, and fasten off the yarn. Using a contrasting, variegated yarn, work a row of crab stitch edging around each slipper.

topknot

hat with crochet tassel

One large, generous tassel made from crochet chain loops decorates the crown of this hat. This type of tassel is made in a strip, then the base is rolled up and stitched to secure before being applied to the hat.

YOU WILL NEED

- 1 ball of pure wool chunky yarn with approx 100 yds (92 m) per 100 g ball
- Size J (6 mm) and size K (6.5 mm) crochet hooks or sizes needed to achieve gauge
- Yarn needle

FINISHED SIZE

Hat measures 8 in. (20 cm) deep, not including tassel, and 22 in. (56 cm) in circumference and will fit average adult head. Tassel measures 6 in. (15 cm) long.

GAUGE

12 stitches and 6$\frac{1}{2}$ rows to 4 in. (10 cm) measured over double crochet using size J (6 mm) hook or size needed to achieve gauge.

MAKING THE HAT

Crochet the hat following the basic pattern on page 26.

WORKING THE TASSEL

1 Using size J (6 mm) hook and leaving 12-in. (30-cm) yarn tail, make foundation chain of 15 chains and work 4 rows of single crochet. Turn, chain 1 and work 1 single crochet into first stitch.

2 Work 1 single crochet into next stitch and work 30 chains.

3 To close chain into a loop, work a slip stitch into single crochet just worked.

4 Repeat Steps 2 and 3 until there are 9 loops in row, then work 1 single crochet into each of 4 remaining stitches. Fasten off yarn, leaving yarn tail as before.

5 Starting at end without loops, roll crochet strip into tight coil, making sure starting tail is free.

6 Thread ending tail into yarn needle and stitch end of coil in place. Use same tail to work several stitches across end of coil and bring it through near starting tail.

FINISHING THE HAT

Finish the hat following the basic pattern on page 26. Use the yarn tails to stitch the tassel to the crown of the hat.

loopy

hat with looped edging

A pretty crochet edging is made from loops of chain stitches joined at intervals to the edge of the hat. Make the edging in the same yarn as the hat or use a brightly contrasting yarn of similar weight.

YOU WILL NEED

- 1 ball of pure wool chunky yarn with approx 100 yds (92 m) per 100 g ball
- Size I (5.5 mm), size J (6 mm), and size K (6.5 mm) crochet hooks or sizes needed to achieve gauge
- Yarn needle

FINISHED SIZE

Hat measures 8 in. (20 cm) deep, not including edging, and 22 in. (56 cm) in circumference and will fit average adult head.

GAUGE

12 stitches and 6$\frac{1}{2}$ rows to 4 in. (10 cm) measured over double crochet using size J (6 mm) hook.

MAKING THE HAT

Crochet the hat following the basic pattern on page 26, but don't break off the yarn.

Prefer the scarf? **see page 24 for the basic pattern**

WORKING THE EDGING

1 After joining last round of hat with a slip stitch, change to size I (5.5 mm) hook and work 1 chain, then work 1 single crochet stitch into same stitch as slip stitch.

2 Work 6 chains, skip next 3 stitches and insert hook into fourth stitch.

3 Work 1 single crochet stitch into fourth stitch and another into next stitch. Continue around hat, working 6 chains, skipping 3 stitches and working a single crochet stitch into each of next 2 stitches.

4 End last repeat with 1 single crochet stitch then join round by working a slip stitch into first single crochet stitch.

FINISHING THE HAT

Finish the hat following the basic pattern on page 26.

looped scarf

Make the basic scarf, then trim each end with a pretty looped edging. Make each loop six chains long, and join it to the scarf edge with one single crochet stitch, spacing the loops close together along the edge.

zigzag

slippers with felt trim

Felt makes a good edging for crochet as it can be cut into shape easily, feels soft next to the skin, and doesn't fray in wear. Use pinking scissors to pattern the edges of narrow strips of felt, then stitch the felt inside the edge of the slippers.

FINISHED SIZES

To fit sizes Small (to fit up to 9 in./23 cm sole), Medium (to fit up to 10 in./25.5 cm sole) and Large (to fit up to 11 in./28 cm sole). Instructions for Medium and Large sizes are given in square brackets.

GAUGE

14 stitches and 16 rows to 4 in. (10 cm) measured over single crochet using size J (6 mm) hook or size needed to achieve gauge.

YOU WILL NEED

- 2 [2, 3] balls of pure wool chunky yarn with approx 100 yds (92 m) per 100 g ball
- Size J (6 mm) and size K (6.5 mm) crochet hooks or sizes needed to achieve gauge
- Yarn needle
- 9-in. (23-cm) square of felt in contrasting color
- Pinking scissors
- Sewing thread to match yarn color
- Sewing needle

MAKING THE SLIPPERS

Crochet and finish the slippers following the basic pattern on page 25.

APPLYING THE TRIM

1 Measure and cut out ³/₄-in. (2-cm) strips across felt square using sharp scissors. Cut enough strips to fit around edge of each slipper, allowing for an overlap of about ³/₈ in. (1 cm) when joining strips.

2 Cut along 1 long edge of each felt strip with pinking scissors to make zigzag edge.

3 Pin strips inside each slipper so zigzag edge shows above slipper edge by about ¹/₄ in. (5 mm). Stretch slipper edge slightly while pinning strips to allow crochet to stretch slightly in wear.

4 Join strips by overlapping them by about ³/₈ in. (1 cm), cutting strips to fit where necessary.

5 Stitch strips in place using matching sewing thread in sewing needle. Working from right side and taking care to go through both layers, make row of neat running stitches below slip stitch edge of slipper.

felt-trimmed bag

Pinked felt strips make a pretty decoration for the edge of a plain bag. If you choose an acrylic felt, the trim can be washed with the bag and won't shrink. Trimmings made from pure wool felt will shrink and should always be removed before washing.

Tip

Make sure you choose washable, non-shrink felt for trimming your slippers. Otherwise, the decorative edge will shrink and you may not be able to fit into your slippers any more!

chapter 3
fastenings and handles

This chapter features over a dozen fabulous ideas for using a wide range of both **handmade** and **store-bought** handles and fastenings. Crocheted and **braided ties** transform a plain hat into a great winter accessory that you might like to combine with the bag with braided fastenings. **Bamboo handles** make a terrific closure for a chunky bag, and **ball buttons** and **crochet loops** make pretty fastenings for our Copper scarf. Brightly colored **zippers** add a striking, punk touch to the Snappy mittens and buttonhole bag, while the basic slippers become sporty footwear thanks to the addition of **tab fastenings**.

copper

scarf with ball buttons and loops

Crochet a short scarf and make button loops along one edge of it. Cover large wooden beads with crochet to make decorative ball buttons, sew them on the opposite edge of the scarf and fasten to make a cosy muffler.

YOU WILL NEED

- 4 balls of pure wool DK yarn with approx 137 yds (125 m) per 50 g ball
- Size F (4 mm), size J (6 mm), and size K (6.5 mm) crochet hooks or sizes needed to achieve gauge
- Yarn needle
- Split ring markers
- 3 wooden beads, each $^3/_4$ in. (2 cm) in diameter

FINISHED SIZE

Scarf measures $6^1/_4$ in. (16 cm) wide and 43 in. (110 cm) long.

GAUGE

12 stitches and 6 rows to 4 in. (10 cm) over double crochet using size J (6 mm) hook and two strands of yarn held together.

NOTE

The scarf is worked in two strands of yarn held together. Ball buttons are worked with one strand of the same yarn.

WORKING THE SCARF

Crochet and finish the scarf following the basic pattern on page 24, working until the scarf measures 43 in. (110 cm) long.

button and loop bag

A chunky ball button and loop make a secure fastening for a buttonhole bag. Make button and loop in contrasting yarn and position them in the center of the buttonhole edge, directly beneath the handle.

Prefer the bag? **see page 25 for the basic pattern**

MAKING THE BUTTONS AND LOOPS

1 Using size F (4 mm) hook and single strand of yarn, chain 2, then work 4 single crochet into first chain. Without joining the round, work 2 single crochet into each of the 4 stitches made on previous round.

2 Continue working in single crochet, shaping cover by working 2 single crochet stitches into every alternate stitch until piece is large enough to cover half of bead.

3 Place cover on bead and start decreasing. Work 1 single crochet into next stitch then work next 2 stitches together. Repeat until bead is almost covered, then work every 2 stitches together until cover is complete.

4 Fasten off yarn, leaving tail of about 12 in. (30 cm). Thread tail into yarn needle and work a few stitches to secure cover. Don't cut tail, because you'll need this later to sew button onto scarf.

5 Mark position of 3 loops on wrong side of scarf. Place first marker 9 rows up from end of scarf and 2 more markers 2 rows apart.

6 Join single yarn to wrong side of scarf at marker with size F (4 mm) hook, work 1 single crochet into scarf at same place and work loop of 8 chains. Secure loop to scarf by working 1 single crochet at second marker. Repeat to make 2 remaining loops and turn work.

7 Work chain 1, then work 1 single crochet into first stitch, 8 single crochet into first loop, and 1 single crochet into stitch between loops. Repeat to complete 3 loops, then sew buttons onto opposite edge of scarf to correspond with loops.

erica

scarf with strip closure

This short scarf fastens with
an ingenious crocheted tab.
Tuck the plain end of the scarf
behind the tab and adjust it to
get a nice snug fit around
your neck.

YOU WILL NEED

- 2 balls of pure wool chunky yarn with approx 100 yds (92 m) per 100 g ball
- Leftovers of the same yarn in contrasting color
- Size I (5.5 mm), size J (6 mm), and size K (6.5 mm) crochet hooks or sizes needed to achieve gauge
- Yarn needle

FINISHED SIZE

Scarf measures 6 in. (15 cm) wide and 40 in. (102 cm) long.

GAUGE

12 stitches and 6 rows to 4 in. (10 cm) over double crochet using size J (6 mm) hook or size needed to achieve gauge.

WORKING THE SCARF

Work and finish the scarf following the basic pattern on page 24.

Tip

To get a snug fit, make sure the strip is slightly shorter than the scarf width. Take the time to try on the scarf after you've pinned the strip in place and adjust if necessary.

MAKING THE STRIP CLOSURE

1 Using size I (5.5 mm) hook and contrasting yarn, make a slip knot on hook 16 in. (40 cm) from end of yarn.

2 Chain 5, then work 1 single crochet into second chain from hook. Work 1 single crochet into each remaining chain. (4 sc)

3 Turn, chain 1 and work 1 single crochet into each stitch of previous row. Repeat this row until strip reaches across width of scarf when slightly stretched. Fasten off yarn, leaving 16-in. (40-cm) tail.

4 Pin strip in place about one third of way down scarf. Try scarf on to check fit and adjust position of strip if necessary.

5 Using yarn tails, stitch each end of strip to scarf and fasten off ends securely on wrong side.

GAUGE

14 stitches and 16 rows to 4 in. (10 cm) measured over single crochet using size J (6 mm) hook or size needed to achieve gauge.

WORKING THE BAG

Crochet the bag following the basic pattern on page 25 until you reach the buttonhole row, ending with a right side row. Do not break off the yarn.

orient

bag with bamboo handles

Ready-made natural bamboo handles look great with a dark green crocheted bag. However, to give the bag a different look, cut two lengths of untreated bamboo cane, paint them with dabs of color, then seal the paint with a final coat of matte or eggshell varnish.

YOU WILL NEED

- 2 balls of pure wool chunky yarn with approx 100 yds (92 m) per 100 g ball
- Size I (5.5 mm), size J (6 mm), and size K (6.5 mm) crochet hooks or sizes needed to achieve gauge
- Yarn needle
- Pair of straight bamboo handles 12 in. (30 cm) long
- Small hand saw

FINISHED SIZE

Bag measures 10$\frac{1}{2}$ in. (26.5 cm) deep, including handles, and 11 in. (28 cm) wide.

Prefer the shallow bag? see page 25 for the basic pattern

shallow bag

Square wooden doweling finished with two coats of matching acrylic paint makes a substantial pair of handles for a shallow bag. Make the bag as given above, but work fewer rows before making the handle strips.

ATTACHING THE HANDLES (BACK AND FRONT ALIKE)

1 To make first handle strip, change to size I (5.5 mm) hook and continue working along top edge. Turn, chain 1 and work 1 single crochet into each of next 10 stitches.

2 Turn, chain 1 and work 1 single crochet into each of 10 stitches made on previous row. Working on these 10 stitches only, work 13 more rows of single crochet, ending with WS row. Fasten off yarn, leaving 12-in. (30-cm) tail.

3 With WS of crochet facing, rejoin yarn to top edge 10 stitches in from side edge. Chain 1 and work 1 single crochet into each of 10 stitches to side edge. Working on these 10 stitches

only, work 14 more rows of single crochet to match first handle strip. Fasten off yarn leaving tail as before.

4 Lay handles across handle strips and mark the length of each handle. Handles should be about $1/2$ in. (1 cm) shorter than width of bag. Cut handles to size with hand saw.

5 With wrong sides of handle strips facing, fold strips in half onto wrong side of bag and pin in place. Using yarn tail, stitch end of strip to bag and stitch outside edges of strip together.

6 Slot handles into strips and stitch inside edges of strip together below each handle.

FINISHING THE BAG
Finish the bag as given in the basic pattern on page 25, ending each side seam about $1/2$ in. (1 cm) below the beginning of the handle strips.

hearts

bag with grab handles

Work the basic buttonhole bag without the buttonholes and attach sturdy grab handles to make a useful tote. Heart buttons stitched through both bag and handles add a decorative touch.

YOU WILL NEED

- 2 balls of pure wool Icelandic Lopi yarn with approx 109 yds (100 m) per 100 g ball
- Size I (5.5 mm), size J (6 mm), and size K (6.5 mm) crochet hooks or sizes needed to achieve gauge
- Yarn needle
- 4 heart-shaped buttons
- Embroidery floss to match yarn color
- Tapestry needle

FINISHED SIZE

Bag measures 11 in. (28 cm) deep, not including handles, and 12 in. (30 cm) wide. Attached handles are approximately 9$\frac{1}{2}$ in. (24 cm) long.

GAUGE

11 stitches and 13 rows to 4 in. (10 cm) measured over single crochet, using size J (6 mm) crochet hook.

WORKING THE BAG

Omitting the buttonhole, crochet and finish the bag following the basic pattern on page 25.

MAKING THE HANDLES
(make two)

With the same yarn and size I (5.5 mm) hook, make a foundation of four chains, leaving a 15-in. (38-cm) yarn tail. Work in single crochet until strip measures about 10 in. (25 cm) ending with a right side row. Cut yarn, leaving a 15 in. (38 cm) yarn tail, and pull tail through loop on hook to finish.

Prefer the shoulder bag? **see page 25 for the basic pattern**

APPLYING THE HANDLES

1 Mark position of handles on bag front. Counting along top edge of crochet, insert 2 markers, each one 8 stitches away from side edges. Markers show position of outer edge of handle.

2 Pin ends of handle to bag front, making sure top edge of front piece overlaps handle ends by about 1 in. (2.5 cm) and outer edges of handle aligns with markers.

3 Using yarn tails, backstitch ends of handle to bag front by sewing through bag below top row of stitches. Work 2 or 3 rows of stitches to make sure handle is firmly fixed. Repeat to match on bag back.

4 Thread floss into tapestry needle and secure on wrong side of handle by working several small stitches into crochet below backstitched line. Holding button in desired position with your thumb, bring floss to right side through both layers and through a hole in button. Take floss back through second hole in button and back to front through first hole. Make several more stitches until button is secure, then take needle through to wrong side and work 2 or 3 stitches through crochet at back of button to secure end. Repeat with remaining 3 buttons.

shoulder bag

Make and finish the bag as described left, then make a single crochet shoulder strap worked on a foundation of seven chains and about 68 in. (173 cm) long. Felt the bag and the strap separately (see pages 114 and 115) and allow to dry. Stitch the ends of the strap to the bag and decorate with leaf-shaped buttons.

Tip

Any shape of button will work on this plain bag. Choose sew-through type buttons and stitch them on securely, taking the stitches through both layers of crochet.

lauren

clutch bag with triangular flap

A simple triangular flap graces this version of the basic bag. Fasten the clutch bag with a pretty brooch or use one of the other fastenings in this chapter, such as a ball button and loop (Copper, page 56) or pair of crochet braids (Anna, page 70).

YOU WILL NEED

- 2 balls of pure wool chunky yarn with approx 100 yds (92 m) per 100 g ball
- Size J (6 mm) and size K (6.5 mm) crochet hooks or sizes needed to achieve gauge
- Split ring markers
- Yarn needle

FINISHED SIZE

Bag measures 7 in. (18 cm) deep and 11 in. (28 cm) wide. Flap measures approximately 4 in. (10 cm) deep when folded over front.

GAUGE

14 stitches and 16 rows to 4 in. (10 cm) measured over single crochet using size J (6 mm) hook or size needed to achieve gauge.

WORKING THE BAG

Crochet the bag front following the basic pattern on page 25 until you have worked 25 rows of single crochet, ending with a right side row. Fasten off yarn.

Crochet the bag back in the same way, but do not break off yarn. Continue as shown at right.

Tip

Fasten the flap with a decorative pin, as shown, or change the look with one of the other fastenings shown in this chapter. To make a plain fastening, either sew a large snap or strips of hook-and-loop tape under the flap.

WORKING THE FLAP

1 Place marker at each end of row you have just worked. Markers indicate position of top edge of front bag piece.

2 Work 3 more rows of single crochet above markers, ending with wrong side row.

3 On next row, chain 1 and start shaping flap. Decrease 1 stitch at beginning of row by working 1 single crochet into first stitch then skipping second stitch. Continue working across row in single crochet until 2 stitches remain at end of row.

4 To decrease 1 stitch at end of row, skip next stitch and work single crochet into last stitch.

5 Repeat Steps 3 and 4 on every row until 4 stitches remain, then fasten off yarn.

6 Pin front and back pieces together, right sides facing and with top edge of front piece aligning with markers on back piece. Stitch side and base seams following the method given for basic bag on page 27. After turning bag to right side, fold flap onto front and secure with brooch.

toggle

mittens with toggle fastening

Toggles make an attractive and interesting alternative to button fastenings. They are inexpensive and available in a range of colors, shapes, and materials including natural wood, faux horn, and colorful plastic and resin.

YOU WILL NEED

- 2 [2, 2] balls of pure wool chunky yarn with approx 100 yds (92 m) per 100 g ball
- Size H (5 mm), size I (5.5 mm), and size J (6 mm) crochet hooks or sizes needed to achieve gauge
- Yarn needle
- Split ring marker
- 2 toggles with 2 holes

FINISHED SIZES

To fit sizes Small (to fit up to 8 in./20 cm around hand), Medium (to fit up to 9 in./23 cm around hand), and Large (to fit up to 10 in./25.5 cm around hand). Instructions for Medium and Large sizes are given in square brackets.

GAUGE

14 stitches and 16 rows to 4 in. (10 cm) measured over single crochet using size J (6 mm) hook or size needed to achieve gauge.

WORKING THE MITTENS

Crochet and finish the mittens following the basic pattern on pages 28–29 omitting sewing the cuff seam.

Tip

Toggles come in lots of shapes, sizes, and materials. Small toggles work best for fastening mittens; choose ones made from faux horn, resin, natural wood, or brightly colored plastic.

Prefer the bag? **see page 25 for the basic pattern**

APPLYING THE TOGGLE

1 Using size H (5 mm) hook and leaving yarn tail of 12 in. (30 cm), chain 10 and fasten off yarn, leaving 12-in. (30-cm) tail.

2 Thread 1 yarn tail into yarn needle and thread chain through 2 holes in toggle. Gently pull chain ends so toggle sits at center of chain and chain ends are level.

3 Following steps on page 57, make button loop on back cuff of mitten large enough to accommodate toggle.

4 Use yarn tails to stitch chain ends to front cuff of mitten, positioning toggle to correspond with loop.

toggle bag

Make a clutch bag in the same way as Lauren on page 64, but make a rectangular flap by omitting the triangular shaping and fasten it with a chunky matching toggle. The toggle on our bag has one hole, unlike the toggle on the mitten, which has two.

snappy

shortie mittens with decorative zipper

Brighten up a shortie mitten by stitching a brightly-colored zipper down the center of the back. Use big, bold stitches and six strands of embroidery floss in a contrasting color for an eye-catching effect.

YOU WILL NEED

- 2 [2, 2] balls of pure wool chunky yarn with approx 100 yds (92 m) per 100 g ball
- Size J (6 mm) and size K (6.5 mm) crochet hooks or sizes needed to achieve gauge
- Yarn needle
- Split ring marker
- 4-in. (10-cm) lightweight dress zipper in a bright color
- Embroidery floss in contrasting color
- Crewel needle large enough to accommodate 6 strands of floss

FINISHED SIZES

To fit sizes Small (to fit up to 8 in./20 cm around hand), Medium (to fit up to 9 in./23 cm around hand), and Large (to fit up to 10 in./25.5 cm around hand). Instructions for Medium and Large sizes are given in square brackets.

GAUGE

14 stitches and 16 rows to 4 in. (10 cm) measured over single crochet using size J (6 mm) hook or size needed to achieve gauge.

WORKING THE MITTENS

Using size K (6.5 mm) hook, ch 24 [26, 27]. Change to size J (6 mm) hook.

ROW 1: 1 sc into 2nd ch from hook, 1 sc into each ch to end, turn. (23 [25, 26] sts)

ROW 2: Ch 1, 1 sc into each sc to end, turn.

Rep Row 2 another 2 [2, 4] times, ending with a WS row.

Change to following the basic pattern on pages 28–29, working from "Shape thumb gusset" to end.

Prefer the bag? **see page 25 for the basic pattern**

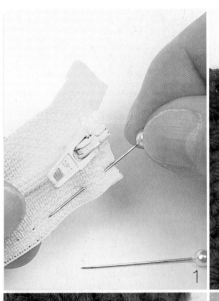

APPLYING THE ZIPPER

1 Turn tape edges at pull end of zipper to wrong side and secure with pins.

2 On right side of mitten and with folded tape aligning with cuff edge, pin closed zipper down center of back.

3 Using 6 strands of floss in crewel needle, stitch zipper in place with large straight stitches placed at right angles to zipper edge.

4 To finish, work 1 or 2 stitches at either side of zipper pull to secure fold to cuff edge.

FINISHING THE MITTENS
Finish the mittens as given in the basic pattern.

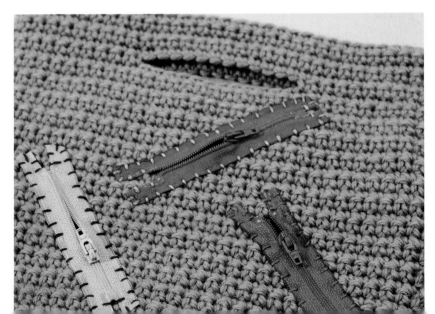

punk bag

Zippers work well as a bag decoration. Choose lightweight dress zippers in a range of contrasting colors or match the zippers to the color of the bag. For example, try black zippers with shiny metal teeth against felted black or dark-colored wool.

anna

hat with crochet braids

Crochet braids are a great way to use up odd lengths of yarn from your stash. You can crochet the chains in different colors of smooth medium-weight yarn or combine other thicknesses and textures.

YOU WILL NEED

- 2 balls of pure wool DK yarn with approx 137 yds (125 m) per 50 g ball in main color
- Leftovers of DK yarn in 3 contrasting colors
- Size F (4 mm), size J (6 mm), and size K (6.5 mm) crochet hooks or sizes needed to achieve gauge
- Yarn needle
- Split ring marker

MAKING THE BRAIDS

1 Using size F (4 mm) hook and 1 color of contrasting yarn, make 2 lengths of chain each 175 chains long, leaving a 12-in. (30-cm) yarn tail at each end. Repeat, making 2 lengths of chain with each of the 2 remaining yarn colors.

2 Mark position of braid at each side of hat with a stitch marker. Thread 3 chains (1 of each color) through hat at marked point, using yarn needle to thread each chain separately.

3 When all 3 chains have been threaded through, adjust so ends are level. Divide with your fingers into 3 groups of 2 chains of same color.

4 Braid chain together, working at alternate sides and moving each outside pair of chains into center of braid. Continue braiding until about 4 in. (10 cm) of each chain is left.

5 Tie end of braid in overhand knot, making sure knot is close to end of braiding. Darn in ends and trim excess yarn.

1

Prefer the bag? see page 25 for the basic pattern

FINISHED SIZE

Hat measures 8 in. (20 cm) deep and 22 in. (56 cm) in circumference and will fit average adult head. Braids measure 12 in. (30 cm) long.

GAUGE

12 stitches and $6^{1}/_{2}$ rows to 4 in. (10 cm) measured over double crochet using two strands of yarn held together and size J (6 mm) hook.

NOTE

The hat is worked with two strands of yarn in main color held together throughout. Braids are worked with one strand of yarn.

MAKING THE HAT

Crochet and finish the hat following the basic pattern on page 26.

braided bag

Pairs of crochet braids make unusual fastenings for a bag. Make two long crochet braids as described below, attaching them to the top of a buttonhole bag at each side of the handle. Knot the braids together to fasten the bag, or make the braid a few inches longer and tie each pair in a floppy bow.

flapper

hat with earflaps

This hat is great fun to wear and gives you more than one look, depending on how you choose to wear it. Leave the earflaps and cords loose, tying the cords together under your chin to keep your ears covered, or knot them on top of your head to make a deerstalker hat.

YOU WILL NEED

■ 1 ball of pure wool chunky yarn with approx 100 yds (92 m) per 100 g ball

■ Size I (5.5 mm), size J (6 mm), and size K (6.5 mm) crochet hooks or sizes needed to achieve gauge

■ Split ring marker

■ Yarn needle

FINISHED SIZE

Hat measures 8 in. (20 cm) deep and 22 in. (56 cm) in circumference and will fit average adult head.

GAUGE

12 stitches and 6$\frac{1}{2}$ rows to 4 in. (10 cm) measured over double crochet using size J (6 mm) hook or size needed to achieve gauge.

MAKING THE HAT

Crochet and finish the hat following the basic pattern on page 26.

basic pattern on page 26.

Tip

If you want to make longer earflaps than shown, work a few more rows of crochet at the start of each flap before beginning the shaping.

MAKING THE EARFLAPS

1 Try on finished hat and mark positions of front of earflaps with markers. Take off hat and insert markers for back of each earflap into eighth stitch back from first markers.

2 With right side of hat facing and using size I (5.5 mm) hook, join yarn into stitch at right marker. Chain 1 and work 1 single crochet into same stitch.

3 Work 1 single crochet into each stitch up to left marker. Working on these 9 stitches only, work 7 more rows of single crochet, ending with wrong side row.

4 Shape lower part of earflap. Work chain 1, work first 2 single crochet stitches together, continue in single crochet until 2 stitches remain, work these 2 stitches together. Repeat this row twice more until 3 stitches remain.

5 Work chain 1, then work 3 stitches together to leave 1 stitch on hook. Working on this stitch, chain 30 and fasten off yarn, leaving 7-in. (18-cm) tail.

6 Cut 6 lengths of yarn 14 in. (36 cm) long. Thread 3 strands in yarn needle and through last chain. Tie strands in overhand knot just below end of chain and trim yarn ends to make neat tassel.

sporty

slippers with tab fastening

Give your slippers a sporty look by making a tab fastening across the instep. Fasten the tabs with squares of hook-and-loop tape so they are a snug fit without being too tight.

YOU WILL NEED

- 2 [2, 3] balls of pure wool chunky yarn with approx 100 yds (92 m) per 100 g ball
- Size I (5.5 mm), size J (6 mm), and size K (6.5 mm) crochet hooks or sizes needed to achieve gauge
- Yarn needle
- 2 split ring markers
- Small piece of hook-and-loop tape ³/₄ in. (2 cm) wide
- Sewing thread to match yarn color
- Sewing needle

FINISHED SIZES

To fit sizes Small (to fit up to 9 in./23 cm sole), Medium (to fit up to 10 in./25.5 cm sole) and Large (to fit up to 11 in./28 cm) sole). Instructions for Medium and Large sizes are given in square brackets.

GAUGE

14 stitches and 16 rows to 4 in. (10 cm) measured over single crochet worked with size J (6 mm) hook or size needed to achieve gauge.

Prefer the bag? see page 25 for the basic pattern

MAKING THE SLIPPERS

Crochet and finish the slippers following the basic pattern on page 27.

tab bag

Two contrasting tabs make a stylish fastening for a plain bag. Stitch one end of each tab to the buttonhole edge on the bag back and secure the other end of the tabs with hook-and-loop tape stitched onto the back of the tabs and front of the bag.

MAKING THE TABS

1 Using size I (5.5 mm) hook, chain 5, leaving yarn tail of 12 in. (30 cm) at beginning.

2 Work 1 single crochet into second chain from hook and 1 single crochet into each remaining chain. Continue working in single crochet on these 4 stitches until tab measures 6 [6$\frac{1}{2}$, 7] in. (15 [16.5, 18] cm). Fasten off yarn.

3 Pin chain edge of tab about halfway down each slipper towards sole. Remembering that this side of slipper goes on inside of foot, try on slippers to check tab position and adjust if necessary. Pin other ends of tabs on other sides of slippers, mark positions and remove pins.

4 Using yarn tail threaded in yarn needle, stitch chain edge of each tab securely to slippers.

5 Cut 2 squares of hook-and-loop tape. Stitch loop piece of each square onto wrong side of each tab using matching sewing thread in sewing needle. Stitch hook pieces onto right sides of slippers to correspond with markers.

chapter 4
beading and embellishing

In chapter 4 we explore the potential for adding **decorative details** to the basic patterns. All five accessories lend themselves well to the addition of **jewel trims** and **sparkling beads**, **buttons**, and **novelty charms**. We show how beads can be attached to the surface of finished accessories and crocheted in. White **snowflake sequins** look fabulous arranged on a felted buttonhole bag, while chunky beads make a fun finish for a fringed scarf. In Nordic, **natural wooden buttons** transform a felted bag into a purse for every occasion. But this chapter is not just about buttons and beads: turn to page 94 for our **curlicue-trimmed** hat and scarf.

elegant

scarf with crocheted-in beads

Clear and pastel-colored chunky beads with a sprinkling of glitter sparkle delicately against a soft green scarf. The beads are crocheted in as you work, so remember to thread them onto the yarn before you start to crochet. You might want to choose metallic beads to decorate a scarf crocheted in a richer yarn color.

YOU WILL NEED

- 6 balls of pure wool DK yarn with approx 137 yds (125 m) per 50 g ball
- Size J (6 mm) and size K (6.5 mm) crochet hooks or sizes needed to achieve gauge
- 128 glitter pony beads $1/4$ in. (8 mm) diameter in assorted colors
- Yarn needle small enough to pass through holes in beads

FINISHED SIZE

Scarf measures 6 in. (15 cm) wide and 54 in. (137 cm) long.

GAUGE

14 stitches and 16 rows to 4 in. (10 cm) over single crochet using size J (6 mm)

hook and two strands of main yarn held together.

NOTE

The scarf is worked with two strands of DK yarn held together throughout. Bead colors are random. Thread all the beads onto the first two balls of yarn. As each ball of yarn is used up, knot the next ball onto the end and slide the beads along past the knot. When the crochet is finished, undo the knots and darn the yarn ends on the wrong side of the scarf.

WORKING THE SCARF

Work the foundation chain for the scarf following the basic pattern on page 24. Work the scarf throughout in single

crochet following the beading pattern below.

FOUNDATION ROW: (RS) 1 sc into 2nd ch from hook, 1 sc into each ch to end, turn.

ROWS 1 and 2: Ch 1, 1 sc into each sc to end, turn.

ROW 3: (WS bead row) Ch 1, 1 sc into each of next 4 sc, *add bead, 1 sc into each of next 5 sc; rep from * to last 5 sts, add bead, 1 sc into each of next 4 sc, turn.

ROWS 4, 5, and 6: Rep Row 2.

ROW 7: (WS bead row) Ch 1, 1 sc into first sc, *add bead, 1 sc into each of next 5 sc; rep from * to last 2 sts, add bead, 1 sc into last sc, turn.

ROWS 8, 9, and 10: Rep Row 2.

Rep Rows 3–10 until all beads are used, ending with a Row 6.

WORKING THE BEADING

1 Holding 2 strands of yarn together, thread beads onto both strands using suitable size of needle. Push beads down yarn for several yards to leave enough yarn to work foundation chain and first few rows of pattern.

2 On bead rows (wrong side rows), work to position of first bead. Slide bead down yarn until it rests snugly against right side of work.

3 Keeping bead in position, insert hook into bead stitch and wrap yarn around hook so there are 2 loops on hook.

4 Wrap yarn over hook again and draw it through to complete stitch. Continue adding beads in same way across row, following pattern instructions.

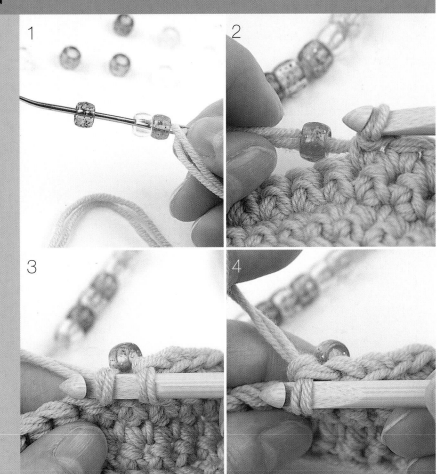

pyramid

scarf with beaded felt circles

Simple, geometric shapes work best for felt appliqué. Decorate each end of a scarf with bright circles of color and contrasting beads, arranging the felt shapes to make a geometric pattern as shown or scatter them in a less structured way.

YOU WILL NEED

- 2 balls of pure wool chunky yarn in main color (MC) with approx 100 yds (92 m) per 100 g ball
- 1 ball of the same yarn in contrasting color (CC)
- Size J (6 mm) and size K (6.5 mm) crochet hooks or sizes needed to achieve gauge
- Yarn needle
- 12-in. (30-cm) square of felt
- Embroidery floss to match felt color
- 108 decorative frosted-finish beads in a contrasting color
- Crewel needle small enough to go through holes in beads

FINISHED SIZE

Scarf measures 6 in. (15 cm) wide and 40 in. (102 cm) long.

GAUGE

12 stitches and 6 rows to 4 in. (10 cm) over double crochet using size J (6 mm) hook or size needed to achieve gauge.

WORKING THE SCARF

Crochet and finish the scarf following the basic pattern on page 24.

Prefer the hat? **see page 26 for the basic pattern**

APPLYING THE DECORATION

1 Draw 12 circles onto felt using an empty paper towel roll or similar object to trace around. Circles should be about 1³/₄ in. (4.5 cm) in diameter. Cut out circles.

2 Pin 6 circles at each end of scarf, arranging them in a pyramid shape (as shown) or more randomly.

3 Thread 3 strands of floss in crewel needle and secure end by working a few stitches through crochet under felt. Work series of straight stitches around outside of each circle to secure it to scarf.

4 Using same thread, stitch a ring of 8 beads on each felt circle following outline of circle and making sure stitches go through felt and crochet. Finish by stitching 1 bead in center of ring, taking thread through to wrong side to secure end.

appliqué hat

Small felt circles decorated with single beads are arranged to make a band of color and texture around a plain hat. Make sure you use a separate length of floss to stitch down each circle so that the hat can stretch around your head.

Tip

Trim the scarf with washable felt so the decorations don't shrink when washed.

81

paris

scarf with beaded fringe

It's quick and easy to add gorgeous beaded fringes to scarves and other accessories. Use chunky plastic craft beads as they are light in weight, unbreakable, and come in a wide range of shapes and colors.

YOU WILL NEED

- 2 balls of pure wool chunky yarn with approx 100 yds (92 m) per 100 g ball
- Size J (6 mm) and size K (6.5 mm) crochet hooks or sizes needed to achieve gauge
- 150 chunky transparent plastic beads in assorted shapes and colors with holes large enough to accommodate yarn
- Yarn needle

FINISHED SIZE

Scarf measures 6 in. (15 cm) wide and 40 in. (102 cm) long, not including the fringe.

GAUGE

12 stitches and 6 rows to 4 in. (10 cm) over double crochet using size J (6 mm) hook or size needed to achieve gauge.

WORKING THE SCARF

Work and finish the scarf following the basic pattern on page 24.

Prefer the bag? **see page 25 for the basic pattern**

MAKING THE BEADED FRINGE

1 Cut 15 lengths of yarn, each 24-in. (30-cm) long, for each end of scarf. Thread 1 length into yarn needle and insert 1 end of yarn into scarf edge.

2 Unthread needle and pull yarn through knitting until ends are level. Tie overhand knot in yarn close to scarf edge. Repeat, spacing remaining 14 lengths evenly along edge.

3 Thread 1 bead onto 1 strand of yarn and tie overhand knot in both strands below bead to secure it. Use yarn needle to help adjust position of knots. Repeat, adding 4 more beads.

4 When all beads have been added, trim ends of yarn neatly about 1 in. (2.5 cm) below final beads.

glitzy bag

Make the basic buttonhole bag pattern and fringe the bottom, adding colorful pink and red heart-shaped beads to make the ultimate girly accessory. The hearts are made from unbreakable plastic and come in plain, transparent, glitter and pearlized finishes.

snowflake

felted bag with sequins

Snowflake-shaped sequins add instant winter glamor to the simplest of knitted accessories. Stitch them onto a felted bag with embroidery floss, securing the center of each sequin with a tiny bead, then work stitches across the arms of the snowflakes to hold them in place.

YOU WILL NEED

- 2 balls of pure wool Icelandic Lopi yarn with approx 109 yds (100 m) per 100 g ball
- Size J (6 mm) and size K (6.5 mm) crochet hooks or sizes needed to achieve gauge
- Yarn needle
- Iridescent white snowflake-shaped sequins, each 1 in. (2.5 cm) in diameter
- Size 11 seed beads to match yarn color
- Embroidery floss to match sequin color
- Crewel needle small enough to pass through holes in beads

FINISHED SIZE

Bag measures 10 in. (25 cm) deep and 10 1/4 in. (26 cm) wide after felting.

GAUGE

Working to an exact gauge is not necessary when making a felted bag. Crochet a gauge swatch using the stated hook size and machine wash it on a hot wash. The crochet fabric should feel thick and substantial and have lost some stitch definition, but still be pliable. You may need to make several swatches using different hooks to get a felted fabric that feels right. There's more information about felting on pages 114 and 115.

WORKING THE BAG

Crochet and finish the bag following the basic pattern on page 25. Felt the bag as described on pages 114 and 115.

Prefer the mittens? **see pages 28–29 for the basic pattern**

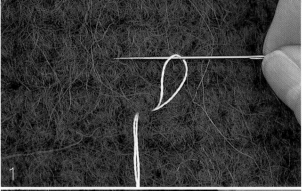

APPLYING THE SEQUINS

1 Cut a 20-in. (50-cm) length of embroidery floss and divide it into single strands. Thread cut ends of 1 strand through crewel needle. On right side of bag front, take needle under 1 crochet stitch and lock thread in place by taking needle through thread loop.

2 Slide 1 snowflake sequin onto thread and take it down thread so it rests on bag. Slide a seed bead onto thread and take needle back through hole in sequin.

3 Work a short straight stitch to secure each arm of snowflake shape, then take needle through to wrong side and secure thread by working several stitches into crochet behind sequin.

4 Repeat Steps 1-3 to secure each snowflake sequin, scattering them at random across front of bag.

glitzy mittens

Sequins come in a huge range of shapes, sizes, and colors and they can be used to add glitz to a pair of plain mittens. Center the sequins on the back of each mitten and stitch them securely in place with embroidery floss.

nordic

felted bag decorated with buttons

A felted bag makes the perfect surface to decorate with a selection of buttons in different shapes and sizes. Choose wooden buttons in a natural finish as shown here or use more colorful ones made from resin or plastic.

YOU WILL NEED

- 2 balls of pure wool Icelandic Lopi yarn with approx 109 yds (100 m) per 100 g ball
- Size I (5.5 mm), size J (6 mm), and size K (6.5 mm) crochet hooks or sizes needed to achieve gauge
- Selection of natural wood buttons
- Embroidery floss to match yarn color
- Yarn needle

FINISHED SIZE

Bag measures 10 in. (25 cm) deep, not including handles, and 10^{1}/$_{4}$ in. (26 cm) wide after felting. Attached handles are approximately 12^{1}/$_{4}$ in. (30 cm) long.

GAUGE

Working to an exact gauge is not necessary when making a felted bag. Crochet a gauge swatch using the stated hook size and machine wash it on a hot wash. The crochet fabric should feel thick and substantial and have lost some stitch definition, but still be pliable. You may need to make several swatches using different hooks to get a felted fabric that feels right. There's more information about felting on pages 114 and 115.

WORKING THE BAG AND HANDLES

Omitting the buttonhole, crochet and finish the bag following the basic pattern on page 25. Make two grab handles (see pages 62–63) using the smallest hook and working on a foundation of five chains. Make each handle about 14 in. (35 cm) long to allow for shrinkage. Felt the bag and the handles separately and allow to dry.

Prefer the scarf? see page 24 for the basic pattern

APPLYING THE HANDLES AND BUTTONS

1 Insert markers about 2 in. (5 cm) from side edges of bag. Pin ends of handle to bag front so handle ends overlap top edge of bag front by about 1 in. (2.5 cm) and outer edges of handle align with markers.

2 Using a 15–in. (38–cm) length of floss in yarn needle, stitch ends of handle securely to bag front. Repeat to attach handles to bag back.

3 Thread floss into yarn needle and secure on right side of bag front by working 2 or 3 small stitches into crochet. Slot a button onto thread and slide it along thread to rest on surface of crochet.

4 Take a stitch over center of button, going back through second hole in button and through crochet. Bring needle through first hole and make

several more stitches until button is secure, then take needle through to wrong side and work 2 or 3 stitches through crochet at back of button to secure end.

5 Repeat Steps 2, 3, and 4 to secure each button, mixing sizes and shapes of buttons and scattering them at random across bag front.

button scarf

Stitch two rows of buttons onto the ends of a plain scarf. We used heart-shaped resin buttons decorated with tartan patterns. Arrange the buttons neatly in rows, as shown, or more randomly for a fun look.

jewel

mittens with jewel trim

Plastic "jewels" are shiny and unbreakable and make great fun trims for crocheted accessories. Each of the square and half-moon shaped jewels used here is drilled with holes, making it easy to stitch them securely in place with matching floss. Arrange the jewels to make a neat pattern on the mitten back.

YOU WILL NEED

- 2 [2, 2] balls of pure wool chunky yarn with approx 100 yds (92 m) per 100 g ball
- Size H (5.5 mm) and size J (6 mm) crochet hooks or sizes needed to achieve gauge
- Yarn needle
- Split ring marker
- Embroidery floss to match yarn color
- Plastic "jewels" with 2 holes: 2 x $^3/_8$ in. (1 cm) squares; 8 x half-moon shapes $^5/_8$ in. (1.5 cm) across
- Crewel needle small enough to fit through holes in jewels

FINISHED SIZES

To fit sizes Small (to fit up to 8 in./20 cm around hand), Medium (to fit up to 9 in./23 cm around hand), and Large (to fit up to 10 in./25.5 cm around hand). Instructions for Medium and Large sizes are given in square brackets.

GAUGE

14 stitches and 16 rows to 4 in. (10 cm) measured over single crochet using size J (6 mm) hook or size needed to achieve gauge.

WORKING THE MITTENS

Crochet the mittens following the basic pattern on pages 28–29.

Prefer the bag? see page 25 for the basic pattern

APPLYING THE JEWELS

1 Cut 20-in (50-cm) length of embroidery floss and divide it into single strands. Thread cut ends of 1 strand through crewel needle. On right side of back of mitten, take needle under 1 crochet stitch and lock floss in place by taking needle through floss loop.

2 Slide 1 square jewel onto floss and take it down floss so it rests on crochet. Work 1 short stitch to secure jewel and take needle through to wrong side. Make 3 or 4 more stitches in same way.

3 Attach other side of jewel in same way. To finish, take needle through to wrong side and secure floss by working several stitches into crochet.

4 Repeat Steps 1–3 to secure each jewel, arranging them in a group to make a pleasing shape. Use a separate piece of floss for each jewel to allow mitten to stretch freely in wear.

FINISHING THE MITTENS
Finish the mittens as given in the basic pattern on pages 28–29.

hearts and stars

Scatter sparkling hearts and stars on the front of a bag crocheted with dark-colored yarn. Add just a few jewels as shown, or combine them with buttons and tiny bells for a more ornate look.

liberty

mittens with shells and bells

Mother-of-pearl shell rings combine well with tiny, gold-colored liberty bells to make unusual bands of decoration on the cuffs of a pair of mittens. Take care to use a separate length of floss to stitch down each trim so the cuffs remain stretchy and comfortable to wear.

YOU WILL NEED

- 2 [2, 2] balls of pure wool chunky yarn with approx 100 yds (92 m) per 100 g ball
- Size H (5.5 mm) and size J (6 mm) crochet hooks or sizes needed to achieve gauge
- Yarn needle
- Split ring marker
- Embroidery floss to match yarn color
- Gold-colored liberty bells
- Flat shell rings $^3/_4$ in. (2 cm) in diameter drilled with 1 hole
- Crewel needle small enough to fit through holes in shell rings

FINISHED SIZES

To fit sizes Small (to fit up to 8 in./20 cm around hand), Medium (to fit up to 9 in./23 cm around hand), and Large (to fit up to 10 in./25.5 cm around hand). Instructions for Medium and Large sizes are given in square brackets.

GAUGE

14 stitches and 16 rows to 4 in. (10 cm) measured over single crochet using size J (6 mm) hook or size needed to achieve gauge.

WORKING THE MITTENS

Crochet the mittens following the basic pattern on pages 28–29.

APPLYING THE SHELLS AND BELLS

1 Cut 20-in. (50-cm) length of embroidery floss and divide it into single strands. Thread cut ends of 1 strand through crewel needle. On right side of cuff where it joins body of mitten, take needle under 1 crochet stitch and lock floss in place by taking needle through floss loop.

2 Slide 1 shell ring onto floss and take it down floss so it rests on crochet. Work 1 short stitch to secure it and take needle through to wrong side. Repeat 2 or 3 times, take needle through to wrong side and secure floss by working several stitches into crochet.

3 Repeat Steps 1 and 2 to secure each ring, arranging them at evenly-spaced intervals around cuff. Use separate piece of floss for each ring to allow cuff to stretch freely in wear.

4 Working in same way, sew 1 bell onto mitten between each shell shape.

FINISHING THE MITTENS

Finish the mittens as given in the basic pattern on pages 28–29.

molly

hat with ring buttons

A ring button is made by
crocheting over a small plastic
ring base. Ring buttons can
be used instead of ordinary
flat buttons to fasten
garments, or as decorative
trims on hats and other
accessories. Make sure that
you leave long yarn tails on
the buttons since you will use
them later to attach the rings
to the hat.

YOU WILL NEED

■ 1 ball of pure wool chunky yarn with
approx 100 yds (92 m) per 100 g ball
■ Leftovers of DK weight yarn in a
contrasting color
■ Size F (4 mm) and J (6 mm) crochet
hooks or sizes needed to achieve
gauge
■ Yarn needle
■ Tapestry needle with eye large enough
to accommodate contrast yarn
■ ³/₄ in. (2 cm) diameter plastic rings

FINISHED SIZE

Hat measures 8 in (20 cm) deep and
22 in. (56 cm) in circumference and will fit
average adult head.

GAUGE

12 stitches and 6¹/₂ rows to 4 in. (10 cm)
measured over double crochet using size
J (6 mm) hook or size needed to achieve
gauge.

MAKING THE HAT

Crochet and finish the hat following the
basic pattern on page 26.

Prefer the mittens? **see pages 28–29 for the basic pattern**

MAKING AND APPLYING THE BUTTONS

1 Work each ring button over a plastic ring. Using thinner yarn and size F (4 mm) hook, make slip knot on hook and insert hook through center of ring. Join yarn by working 1 single crochet stitch over ring.

2 Continue working around ring, making 1 round of 15 or 16 single crochet stitches over it until ring is completely covered. Join the round by working 1 slip stitch into first single crochet stitch.

3 Break off yarn, leaving end of about 15 in. (38 cm) and thread it into tapestry needle. Work 1 row of running stitches through outer loops of crochet.

4 Turning edge of crochet backward to center of ring, draw thread up firmly and secure it with a few stitches on wrong side, but don't break it off. Darn in short yarn end.

5 On back of button, work strands of yarn diagonally across button several times to make a shank. Bring needle to center of button under shank.

6 Spacing buttons evenly around hat, stitch each button in place by working several stitches through center of shank and through hat. Secure yarn end on wrong side of hat.

ring mittens

Ring buttons look attractive when arranged in a line down the back of plain mittens. Choose a smooth yarn to make buttons like the ones shown here, or use a novelty yarn incorporating metallic threads or a pretty, fluffy mohair.

curly

hat with curlicues

Six or more curlicues of crochet make a fun and unusual top knot for a hat. The curlicues are very easy to make because the spiral shape forms naturally as you crochet.

YOU WILL NEED

- 2 balls of pure wool DK yarn with approx 137 yds (125 m) per 100 g ball
- Small amounts of the same yarn in a selection of coordinating colors
- Size F (4 mm), size H (5 mm), size J (6 mm), and size K (6.5 mm) crochet hooks or sizes needed to achieve gauge
- Yarn needle

FINISHED SIZE

Hat measures 8 in. (20 cm) deep, not including edging, and 22 in. (56 cm) in circumference and will fit average adult head. Plain curlicues are approximately $4\frac{1}{4}$ in. (11 cm) long; striped ones are 5 in. (13 cm) long.

GAUGE

12 stitches and $6\frac{1}{2}$ rows to 4 in. (10 cm) measured over double crochet using size J (6 mm) hook and two strands of yarn held together.

MAKING THE HAT

Crochet and finish the hat following the basic pattern on page 26, using two strands of yarn held together.

Prefer the scarf? see page 24 for the basic pattern

1

2

MAKING AND APPLYING THE CURLICUES

1 Using size H (5 mm) hook and a coordinating yarn, work a loose foundation chain of 30 stitches, leaving a 12–in. (30–cm) yarn tail. Change to size F (4 mm) hook and work 2 double crochet stitches into fourth chain from hook. Work 3 double crochet stitches into next chain.

2 Continue along chain working 3 double crochet stitches into each chain. As you work, the crochet strip will begin to twist naturally into a curly spiral formation. At end of row, fasten off yarn and darn in yarn end.

3 To make a striped curlicue, work a plain one in one color of yarn, leaving long ends with which to attach finished curlicue. Join a coordinating yarn to outer edge of top of curlicue and work a row of single crochet stitches along edge. Fasten off ends of coordinating yarn.

4 Make 3 plain and 3 striped curlicues using different shades of yarn. Attach them to crown of hat by threading yarn end of each curlicue through center of crown and securing with a few stitches on wrong side of hat.

3

4

curly scarf

Crochet a plain scarf then decorate each end with a row of curlicues worked in a contrasting yarn color. Space the curlicues evenly along the edge to form a chunky fringe.

charming

slippers with novelty charms

Metal charms and other jewelry components, such as rings and pendants, are useful for decorating accessories. We've chosen pretty silver strawberries and stitched a trio of them onto the front of a pair of slippers using matching thread.

YOU WILL NEED

- 2 [2, 3] balls of pure wool chunky yarn with approx 100 yds (92 m) per 100 g ball
- Size J (6 mm) and size K (6.5 mm) crochet hooks or sizes needed to achieve gauge
- Yarn needle
- 6 silver-colored strawberry charms approx $\frac{5}{8}$ in. (1.5 cm) long
- Embroidery floss to match yarn color
- Crewel needle small enough to go through loop on charm

FINISHED SIZES

To fit sizes Small (to fit up to 9 in./23 cm sole), Medium (to fit up to 10 in./25.5 cm sole) and Large (to fit up to 11 in./28 cm sole). Instructions for Medium and Large sizes are given in square brackets.

GAUGE

14 stitches and 16 rows to 4 in. (10 cm) measured over single crochet using size J (6 mm) hook or size needed to achieve gauge.

MAKING THE SLIPPERS

Crochet and finish the slippers following the basic pattern on page 27.

APPLYING THE CHARMS

1 Cut 20-in. (50-cm) length of embroidery floss and divide it into single strands. Thread cut ends of 1 strand through crewel needle and secure on wrong side of slipper front by working 2 or 3 small stitches into crochet just below slip stitch edge.

2 Bring needle through to right side at center front, just below slip stitch edging.

3 Slide 1 charm onto floss and take it down floss so it rests flat against crochet with loop at top.

4 Take 1 stitch over loop of charm and back through crochet. Repeat 2 or 3 times until charm is securely attached and fasten off floss on wrong side by working 2 or 3 stitches into crochet.

5 Repeat Steps 1–4 to secure each charm, using separate length of floss for each charm and spacing them evenly around slipper front. Repeat on second slipper.

chapter 5

customizing crochet

In this chapter, you'll discover how **substituting yarns** and stitches can transform our five basic patterns. Try using **lacy stitch patterns**, felting the accessories, or decorating them with rows of **surface crochet** to stamp your own style on the pieces. By using some of the ideas from the earlier chapters too—changing edgings of accessories and **embellishing** them with handmade or store-bought trimmings and handles—you can create accessories that are **entirely original** and **unique** to you.

glitter
small evening bag

It's easy to change our basic bag pattern to create a smaller accessory to use in the evening. To make this pretty evening purse, follow the basic bag pattern on page 25, working it in a thinner yarn with a smaller hook, adding contrasting stripes and leaving out the buttonhole. Add a long shoulder strap to finish the purse.

YOU WILL NEED

- 2 balls of metallic silver yarn with approx 92 yds (85 m) per 25 g ball (MC)
- 1 ball of the same yarn in a contrasting color (CC)
- Size F (4 mm) and size G (4.5 mm) crochet hooks or sizes needed to achieve gauge
- Yarn needle

FINISHED SIZE

Bag measures 6 in. (15 cm) deep, not including handles, and 6$^{1}/_{4}$ in. (16 cm) wide. Attached handles are approximately 4 feet (122 cm) long.

GAUGE

20 stitches and 23 rows to 4 in. (10 cm) measured over single crochet, using size F (4 mm) hook or size needed to achieve gauge.

WORKING THE BAG

Omitting the buttonhole, crochet and finish the bag following the basic pattern on page 25, working the 35 rows in this color sequence:

18 rows in MC, 2 rows in CC, 2 rows in MC, 2 rows in CC, 2 rows in MC, 2 rows in CC, 7 rows in MC.

Tip

When working a long strip of crochet, such as a shoulder strap, make more foundation chains than you think you'll need, because the chain gets shorter when the first row of stitches are worked. Unravel any unused chains after the strap is worked.

WORKING THE SHOULDER STRAP

1 Using main yarn and size G (4.5 mm) hook, chain length required for strap plus about one third as much again, because chain will become shorter when stitches are worked into it. (See Tip.)

2 Work 1 single crochet into second chain from hook and work along chain in single crochet until strap is desired length. Turn and work a second row of single crochet in same yarn.

3 Join contrasting yarn, turn and work 2 more rows of single crochet.

4 Join main yarn. Turn and work 2 more rows of single crochet. Fasten off yarn.

happy

stocking hat with pom-poms

Give a fresh and funky new look to a basic hat by adding extra rows of double crochet between the pattern rounds. This elongates the top section and makes a stocking cap. Trim the cap with two or more pom-poms made in contrasting yarn.

YOU WILL NEED

- 4 balls of pure wool DK yarn with approx 137 yds (125 m) per 50 g ball in main color
- 1 ball of the same yarn in 3 contrasting colors
- Size J (6 mm) and size K (6.5 mm) crochet hooks or sizes needed to achieve gauge
- Yarn needle
- Pom-pom maker (or stiff cardstock - see Notes)

FINISHED SIZE

Hat measures 16 in. (41 cm) deep, not including pom-poms, and 22 in. (56 cm) in circumference and will fit average adult head.

GAUGE

12 stitches and $6^{1}/_{2}$ rows to 4 in. (10 cm) measured over double crochet using two strands of yarn held together and size J (6 mm) hook.

NOTES

Two strands of main yarn are held together throughout. To make the pom-poms, buy a set of adjustable plastic pom-pom rings or cut two identical doughnut shapes from sturdy cardstock. If making your own shapes, make the center ring about one quarter of the diameter of the outer ring.

MAKING THE HAT

Working Rounds 1–6 of the basic pattern from page 26, insert extra rows of double crochet between the pattern rounds as follows:

Work Round 1, then work 2 rounds even.
Work Round 2, then work 3 rounds even.
Work Round 3, then work 3 rounds even.
Work Round 4, then work 3 rounds even.
Work Round 5, then work 3 rounds even.
Work Round 6, then work 3 rounds even.
Continue to follow the basic pattern from Round 7 to the end. Finish the hat as given in the basic pattern, then stitch two pom-poms to the top of the hat using the yarn ties.

MAKING POM-POMS (MAKE TWO)

1 Place 2 pom-pom rings (or cardstock circles) back to back. Thread several strands of yarn in yarn needle. Wind yarn around rings, adding further lengths of yarn until center space is tightly filled.

2 Using sharp scissors, carefully cut through yarn strands, easing scissor points right between pom-pom rings.

3 Ease rings apart and tie length of matching yarn firmly around strands in middle of rings.

4 Pull rings apart and ease them off yarn strands. Trim off any uneven pieces of yarn. Leave yarn ties untrimmed, and use to attach pom-poms to hat.

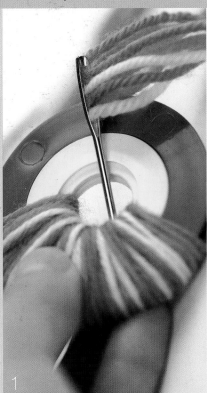

sarah

mesh tote bag

Work the basic buttonhole bag pattern in strong cotton yarn to make a useful tote bag for carrying your shopping. The center section of the bag incorporates an openwork mesh stitch, but using one of the other stitch patterns will give you a different effect.

YOU WILL NEED

- 3 balls of pure cotton DK yarn with approx 92 yds (85 m) per 100 g ball
- Size J (6 mm) and size K (6.5 mm) crochet hooks or sizes needed to achieve gauge
- Yarn needle

FINISHED SIZE

Bag measures 12 in. (30 cm) deep and 10 in. (25 cm) wide.

GAUGE

14 stitches and 16 rows to 4 in. (10 cm) measured over single crochet using size J (6 mm) hook and two strands of main yarn held together.

NOTES

Two strands of yarn are held together throughout. When working with double yarn from an odd number of balls, you'll need to wind off half the yarn in the third ball.

WORKING THE BAG FRONT

Holding 2 strands of yarn together and using size K (6.5 mm) hook, ch 34. Change to size J (6 mm) hook and work Rows 1–4 of the basic bag pattern as given on page 25.
Start mesh pattern
ROW 1: (RS) Ch 4 (counts as 1 dc, ch 1), sk first 2 sc, 1 dc into next sc, *ch 1, sk next sc, 1 dc into next sc; rep from * to end, turn.
ROW 2: Ch 4, sk first dc, 1 dc into next dc, *ch 1, 1 dc into next dc; rep from * to end, working last dc into 3rd of ch-4, turn.

Rep Row 2 ten more times, ending with a WS row.

NEXT ROW: Ch 1, 1 sc into each ch and dc along row, working last 2 sc into 3rd and 4th of ch-4, turn.

NEXT ROW: Ch 1, 1 sc into each sc along row.

Work 3 more rows of sc, then work buttonhole and handle as given for basic

pattern, but working buttonhole over 13 sts to accommodate extra chain made at beginning.

WORKING THE BAG BACK

Work as for front.

FINISHING THE BAG

Finish the bag following the basic pattern on page 25.

STITCH PATTERNS

We used the openwork mesh stitch for the bag. You can substitute either of the other two stitch patterns given here, but remember to adjust the number of stitches in the foundation chain and in the buttonhole according to the multiple of stitches required for pattern you want to work.

1 OPENWORK MESH

Work over a multiple of 2 chains plus 4.
ROW 1: (RS) 1 dc into 6th ch from hook, *ch 1, sk next ch, 1 dc into next ch; rep from * to end, turn.
ROW 2: Ch 4 (counts as 1 dc, ch 1), *1 dc into next dc, ch 1; rep from * to end, working last dc into 2nd of beg skipped ch-5, turn.
ROW 3: Ch 4 (counts as 1 dc, ch 1), *1 dc into next dc, ch 1; rep from * to end, working last dc into 3rd of ch-4, turn.
Rep Row 3 for length required.

2 PLAIN TRELLIS

Work over a multiple of 4 chains plus 2.
ROW 1: 1 sc into 6th ch from hook, *ch 5, sk next 3 chs, 1 sc into next ch; rep from * to end, turn.
ROW 2: *Ch 5, 1 sc into next ch-5 sp; rep from * to end, turn.
Rep Row 2 for length required.

3 TRELLIS WITH SHELLS

Work over a multiple of 12 chains plus 3.
ROW 1: (RS) 2 dc into 4th ch from hook, *sk next 2 chs, 1 sc into next ch, ch 5, sk next 5 chs, 1 sc into next ch, sk next 2 chs, 5 dc into next ch; rep from * to end, working only 3 dc into last ch, turn.
ROW 2: Ch 1, 1 sc into first st, *ch 5, 1 sc into next ch-5 sp, ch 5, 1 sc into 3rd dc of next 5-dc group; rep from * to end, working last sc into 3rd of beg skipped ch-3, turn.
ROW 3: *Ch 5, 1 sc into next ch-5 sp, 5 dc into next sc, 1 sc into next ch-5 sp; rep from * ending with ch 2, 1 dc into last sc, turn.
ROW 4: Ch 1, 1 sc into first st, *ch 5, 1 sc into 3rd dc of next 5-dc group, ch 5, 1 sc into next ch-5 sp; rep from * to end, turn.
ROW 5: Ch 3, 2 dc into first st, *1 sc into next ch-5 sp, ch 5, 1 sc into next ch-5 sp, 5 dc into next sc; rep from * to end, working only 3 dc into last sc, turn.
ROW 6: Ch 1, 1 sc into first st, *ch 5, 1 sc into next ch-5 sp, ch 5, 1 sc into 3rd dc of next 5-dc group; rep from * to end, working last sc into 3rd of ch-3, turn.
Rep Rows 3-6 for length required, ending with a Row 5.

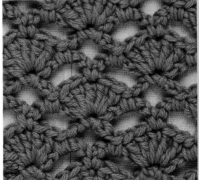

patience

lacy shell scarf

Stitch patterns need a given number of stitches in the foundation chain for the pattern to work correctly. When using a different pattern to crochet a scarf, simply chain the number required and work a long strip. The Patience scarf is worked in Lacy Shell Stitch on a foundation chain of 30 (8 x 3 + 6).

STITCHES

You can use any of the stitches shown here to make our basic scarf. Shell stitches feature groups of three or more stitches that share the same chain, stitch, or chain space, and they look rather like clam shells. Usually, chains or stitches at either side of a shell are skipped to compensate for the shell and each stitch making up a shell is counted as one stitch. Chevron stitches use a sequence of increases and decreases to create zigzag rows and look good worked in one color or in stripes.

STITCH PATTERNS

 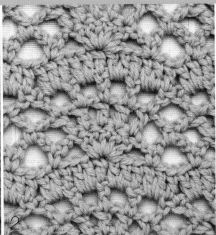 

1 LACY SHELL STITCH

Work a multiple of 8 chains plus 6.

ROW 1: (RS) 1 dc into 6th ch from hook, *sk next 2 chs, 5 dc into next ch, sk next 2 chs, 1 dc into next ch, ch 1, sk next ch, 1 dc into next ch; rep from * to end, turn.

ROW 2: Ch 4 (counts as 1 dc, ch 1), sk first dc, 1 dc into next dc, *5 dc into center st of next 5 dc group, sk next 2 dc, 1 dc into next dc, ch 1, 1 dc into next dc; rep from * working last dc into 4th of beg skipped ch-5, turn.

ROW 3: Ch 4 (counts as 1 dc, ch 1), sk first dc, 1 dc into next dc, *5 dc into center st of next 5 dc group, sk next 2 dc, 1 dc into next dc, ch 1, 1 dc into next dc; rep from * working last dc into 3rd of ch-4, turn.

Rep Row 3 for length required.

Fasten off yarn.

2 SHELL LACE

Work a multiple of 12 chains plus 3.

ROW 1: (RS) 1 dc into 4th ch from hook, 1 dc into each ch to end, turn.

ROW 2: Ch 3, 2 dc into first dc, ch 2, sk next 3 dc, 1 sc into next dc, ch 5, sk next 3 dc, 1 sc into next dc, ch 2, sk next 3 dc, *5 dc into next dc, ch 2, sk next 3 dc, 1 sc into next dc, ch 5, sk next 3 dc, 1 sc into next dc, ch 2, sk next 3 dc; rep from * ending with 3 dc into 3rd of beg skipped ch-3, turn.

ROW 3: Ch 4, sk first dc, 1 dc into next dc, ch 1, 1 dc into next dc, ch 2, sk next ch 2 sp, 1 sc into next ch-5 sp, ch 2, *[1 dc into next dc, ch 1] 4 times, 1 dc into next dc, ch 2, sk next ch 2 sp, 1 sc into next ch-5 sp, ch 2; rep from * to last 2 dc, [1 dc into next dc, ch 1] twice, 1 dc into 3rd of ch 3, turn.

ROW 4: Ch 5, sk first dc, 1 dc into next dc, ch 2, 1 dc into next dc, *sk next sc, [1 dc into next dc, ch 2] 4 times, 1 dc into next dc; rep from * to last sc, sk last sc, [1 dc into next dc, ch 2] twice, 1 dc into 3rd of ch 4, turn.

ROW 5: Ch 3, 2 dc into next ch-2 sp, 1 dc into next dc, 2 dc into next ch-2 sp, sk next dc, 1 dc into next dc, * [2 dc into next ch-2 sp, 1 dc into next dc] 3 times, 2 dc into next ch-2 sp, sk next dc, 1 dc into next dc; rep from * to last ch-2 sp, 2 dc into last ch-2 sp, 1 dc into next dc, 2 dc into sp formed by ch-5, sk first 2 chs of ch-5, 1 dc into 3rd of ch-5, turn.

ROW 6: Ch 3, 2 dc into first dc, ch 2, sk next 3 dc, 1 sc into next dc, ch 5, sk next 3 dc, 1 sc into next dc, ch 2, sk next 3 dc, *5 dc into next dc, ch 2, sk next 3 dc, 1 sc into next dc, ch 5, sk next 3 dc, 1 sc into next dc, ch 2, sk next 3 dc; rep from * ending with 3 dc into 3rd of ch-3, turn.

Rep Rows 3–6 for length required, ending with a Row 5.

3 MINI CHEVRONS

Work a multiple of 10 chains plus 3.

ROW 1: (RS) 1 dc into 4th ch from hook, 1 dc into each of next 4 chs, *sk next 2 chs, 1 dc into each of next 4 chs, ch 2, 1 dc into each of next 4 chs; rep from * to last 6 chs, sk next 2 chs, 1 dc into each of next 3 chs, 2 dc into last ch, turn.

ROW 2: Ch 3, 1 dc into first dc, 1 dc into each of next 3 dc, *sk next 2 dc, 1 dc into each of next 3 dc, [1 dc, ch 2, 1 dc] into next ch-2 sp, 1 dc into each of next 3 dc; rep from * to last 6 dc, sk next 2 dc, 1 dc into each of next 3 dc, 2 dc into 3rd of beg skipped ch-3, turn.

ROW 3: Ch 3, 1 dc into first dc, 1 dc into each of next 3 dc, *sk next 2 dc, 1 dc into each of next 3 dc, [1 dc, ch 2, 1 dc] into next ch-2 sp, 1 dc into each of next 3 dc; rep from * to last 6 dc, sk next 2 dc, 1 dc into each of next 3 dc, 2 dc into 3rd of ch-3, turn.

Rep Row 3 for length required.

cozy

hat with stripes

Simple, clean-cut stripes transform our basic hat into something special. The stripes are worked in four colors, arranged in a repeating sequence of cream, yellow, orange, and brown. On Rounds 1–10, change the yarn color on every round, then work Rounds 11–13 in orange, and finish by working Round 14 in brown.

FUN WITH STRIPES

Once you are familiar with basic crochet techniques and stitches, have fun experimenting with striped variations. Work one-row stripes in a repeating or random color sequence (like the Cozy hat) or vary the depth of the stripes by working varying numbers of rows or rounds in each color. Stripe colors can contrast strongly or the effect can be made more subtle by using a restricted palette of shades of one color plus one or more coordinating colors. Single and double crochet stitches all look good worked in stripes.

1

WORKING STRIPES

1 FELTED BAG WITH LOOP FASTENING

This small bag was also worked in the round using shades of pink tapestry wool highlighted with a single stripe of bright blue. The pretty fastening is made from a twisted strip of felted single crochet stitched to the back of the bag.

2 FELTED BAG WITH SHOULDER STRAP

Worked in a selection of bright, clashing colors, this small bag was worked in rounds of single crochet, rather than in rows. To begin working a bag in the round, make a foundation chain to the desired length and work around both sides of the chain, in the same way as the basic slippers on page 27.

3 FELTED BAG WITH HANDLES

Felting an accessory that has been worked in stripes changes its appearance because neighboring yarn colors blend with each other to create a softer effect. Worked in single crochet, this varation of the bag with grab handles on page 62 was worked using leftovers of tapestry wool and double knitting wool in a wide range of colors. Yarns were joined wherever a length was used up, rather than at the side edges.

2

3

amanda

plastic shoulder bag

Strips cut from plastic grocery bags make a good yarn with which to crochet because they create a strong, hard-wearing fabric. You can crochet the basic bag pattern on page 25 with plastic strips to make a very large tote. Alternatively, here's an adaptation with fewer stitches and rows, and a shoulder strap.

YOU WILL NEED

- 30–40 plastic grocery bags, depending on size
- Size P (12 mm) crochet hook
- Plastic garden twine
- Yarn needle large enough to accommodate thickness of twine

FINISHED SIZE

Bag measures 12 in. (30 cm) deep and 12 in. (30 cm) wide, not including handle.

GAUGE

$3^1/2$ stitches and $5^1/2$ rows to 4 in. (10 cm) measured over single crochet using size P (12 mm) hook.

PREPARING THE YARN

Cut and join the strips as shown at right.

WORKING THE BAG

Ch 16.
Work 17 rows of single crochet until the front measures 12 in. (30 cm), ending with a RS row.
Fasten off yarn.
Work back to match front.

WORKING THE SHOULDER STRAP

Ch 3.
Work even in single crochet until the strap measures approximately 32 in. (81 cm), ending with a WS row.
Fasten off yarn.

FINISHING THE BAG

Place the front and back pieces together with right sides facing and stitch together using plastic twine, taking the needle between individual stitches rather than stitching through the strips. Stitch each end of the strap to the wrong side of the bag, overlapping the edges by about 1 in. (2.5 cm) and stitch them securely in place as above. Turn the bag right side out.

MAKING THE YARN

1 Lay each bag flat and cut off handles and bottom seam using sharp pair of scissors.

2 Fold plastic in half so folded side edges of bag align. Fold in half again to make strip.

3 Starting at one end and cutting through all layers in strip, cut strip into sections about 1–1¹/₂ in. (2.5–4 cm) wide. Open out sections to form rings.

4 To connect rings, loop one over and behind another ring and carefully pull to connect both rings.

5 Pull connected rings to form knot. Pull gently to avoid plastic tearing.

6 Repeat from Step 4, rolling plastic "yarn" into several balls. When making bag, connect end of old ball to new one by looping it in same way as Step 4.

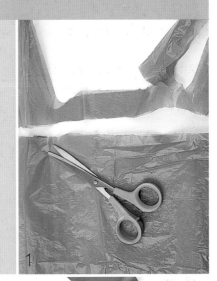

amy

mittens with contrast cuff

In this project, novelty yarn
has been used to add interest
and texture to plain mittens.
Make short mittens without a
cuff (see Fluffy, page 42), then
trim the cuff edge with a band
of single or double crochet
worked with two eyelash yarns
held together.

WORKING WITH NOVELTY YARNS

Novelty yarns come in many textures and
may be a solid color or space-dyed in
attractive color combinations. They can be
used in small amounts as decorative
accents or to replace a smooth yarn when
working a pattern, providing they work up
to the same gauge.

Many novelty yarns are made from a
mixture of fibers and need special care
when washing. (Check the ball or skein
band for the fiber composition and care
details.) These yarns are more difficult to
work with than smooth yarns. Concentrate
and count carefully when crocheting
because it's harder to distinguish
individual stitches than when working with
smooth yarns.

WORKING WITH NOVELTY YARNS

The swatches below give you an idea of the different types of novelty yarns available. Each yarn is contrasted against a smooth chunky yarn made from pure wool.

1 MOHAIR YARN

Mohair yarns are soft and fluffy and contain a high proportion of kid mohair spun around a synthetic core for strength. If you find mohair yarn feels itchy next to the skin, use it in small amounts as a trim rather than to make the main part of an accessory.

2 RIBBON YARN

Ribbon yarns are woven in a flat strip and come in different widths and weights. The yarn in this swatch is made from cotton and nylon and changes color at intervals, shading from blue to plum. The ribbon yarn is held together with a solid-colored smooth yarn to add thickness.

3 TEXTURED YARN

Novelty yarns made from pure wool or wool/synthetic mixtures create a wide range of textures and color combinations. Yarns may be textured with loops, bobbles, and slubs, or be twisted to vary from very fine to very thick at regular intervals along the yarn. The yarn in the swatch is spun mainly from wool with smaller amounts of acrylic and nylon.

4 EFFECT YARN

Effect yarns, or component yarns, come in different fiber combinations and textures to add color and sheen to your work without adding bulk. The swatch shows an effect yarn made from nylon held together with the main chunky yarn.

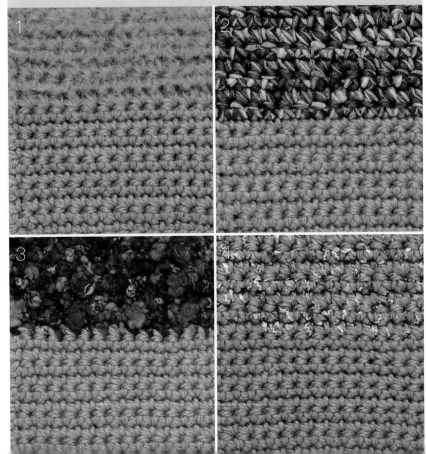

violet

felted bag

These two bags were made from the basic pattern on page 25 using two strands of Shetland double knitting wool held together. The dark purple bag was machine washed in hot water, the light purple bag was not washed so remains unfelted.

FELTING SWATCHES

Felting or—to give the process the correct term—fulling, describes deliberately shrinking a piece of crocheted fabric so that it thickens and becomes solid, yet still pliable. Single crochet gives the best results and the fabric shrinks fairly evenly lengthwise and widthwise. The amount of shrinkage will vary depending on how loosely the piece has been crocheted, the temperature and length of the wash, and the amount of friction. The easiest way to felt something is to machine wash it, adding an old towel or pair of jeans to the machine for extra friction. Pull the wet fabric gently into shape and lay it flat to dry. This may take several days, depending on the weather and the thickness of the felt. Pure wool yarns are used for felting, but avoid those that are treated to be machine washable, as most will not felt. The best types to try are wools labeled as "hand wash only." Some yarns lose stitch definition quickly when washed, while others may need several washes before you get the effect you want. Remember that felting is an inexact science so always crochet a swatch and wash and dry it first before starting to crochet your project. Keep on swatching until you're happy with the results.

1 TWO STRANDS OF SHETLAND WOOL

Single crochet worked in two contrasting colors of Shetland double knitting wool held together. Washed in hot water, this type of wool felts really well, making a thick, even fabric that thickens up nicely.

2 CHUNKY WOOL

Single crochet worked in a pure wool chunky yarn and washed twice in hot water. After the first wash, the fabric was too thin and still showed a lot of stitch definition. After the second hot wash, the yarn had felted a little bit too much, resulting in a hard, rather stiff fabric.

3 ICELANDIC WOOL PLUS RIBBON YARN

Single crochet worked with one strand of light Icelandic wool and one strand of silk/viscose ribbon yarn and washed in hot water. This has a lovely soft finish; the stitch definition is still there but the fabric has thickened up nicely.

4 ICELANDIC WOOL PLUS EYELASH YARN

Single crochet worked with one strand of light Icelandic wool and one strand of synthetic eyelash yarn and washed in hot water. The wool component has felted and shrunk less than the other samples because the contrast yarn won't felt. The fabric is soft yet substantial with a lovely furry surface.

5 ICELANDIC WOOL PLUS MOHAIR

Two-row stripes worked in single crochet using one strand of Icelandic yarn and two strands of solid color mohair yarn and washed in hot water. The felt feels thick and substantial, but is still very soft.

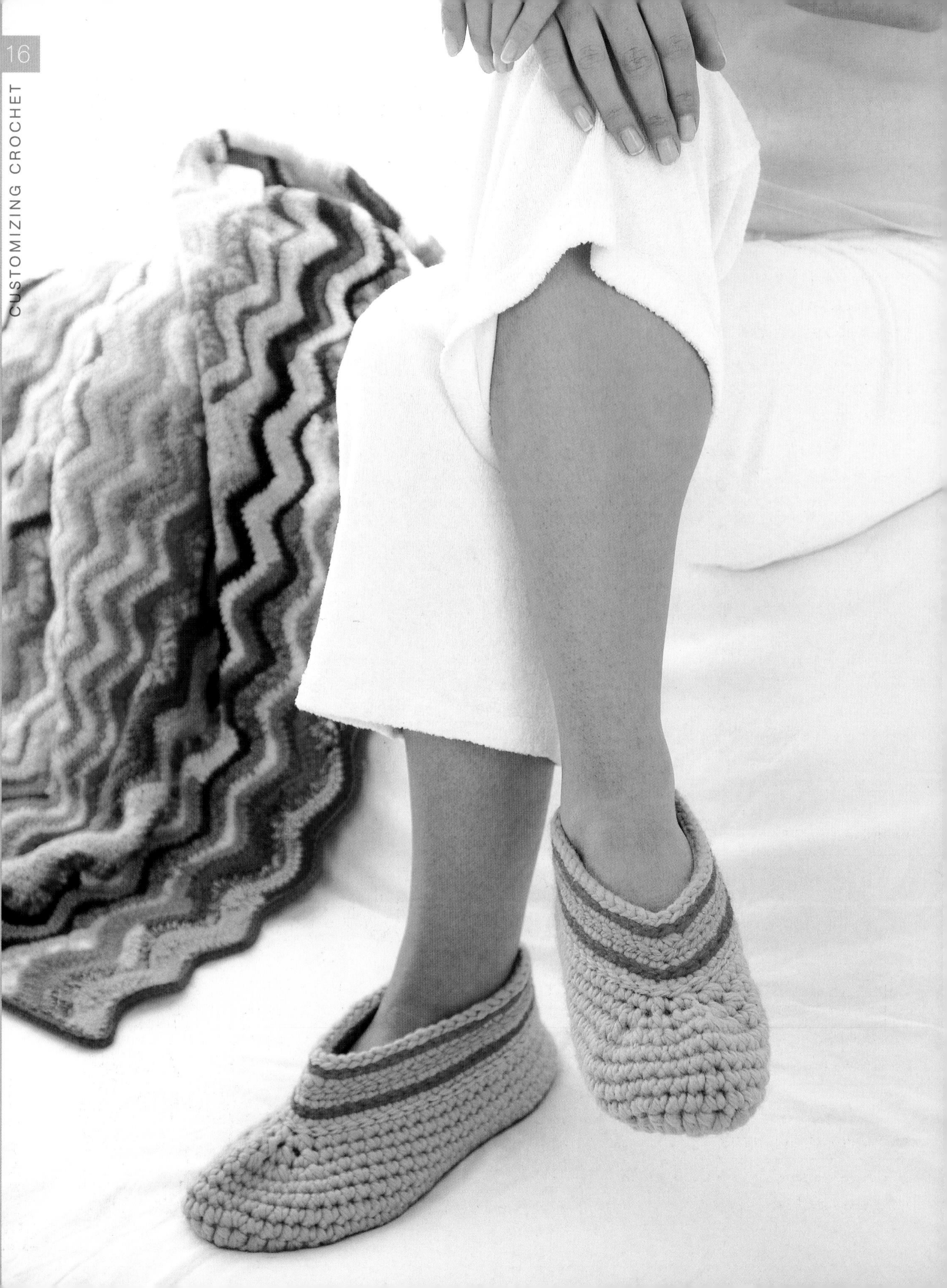

spice

slippers with surface crochet

Surface crochet is a technique that adds decoration to a previously worked crochet background. A round or row of surface crochet looks similar to embroidered chain stitch, but it's worked with a hook through the fabric. Decorate slippers, as shown here, or use rows of surface crochet to add color to a plain buttonhole bag.

YOU WILL NEED

- 2 [2, 3] balls of pure wool chunky yarn with approx 100 yds (92 m) per 100 g ball
- Leftovers of the same weight yarn in 4 contrasting bright colors
- Size H (5 mm), size J (6 mm), and size K (6.5 mm) crochet hooks or sizes needed to achieve gauge
- Yarn needle

FINISHED SIZES

To fit sizes Small (to fit up to 9 in./23 cm sole), Medium (to fit up to 10 in./25.5 cm sole) and Large (to fit up to 11 in./28 cm sole).

GAUGE

14 stitches and 16 rows to 4 in. (10 cm) measured over single crochet worked with size J (6 mm) hook or size needed to achieve gauge.

MAKING THE SLIPPERS

Crochet and finish the slippers following the basic slippers pattern on page 27.

WORKING THE DECORATION

1 Thread 1 of the contrasting yarns in yarn needle. Secure end of yarn on wrong side of slipper back by working 1 or 2 stitches into crochet.

2 Insert size H (5 mm) hook through slipper just below row of slip stitch edging and close to where contrasting yarn is secured. Wrap yarn over hook and pull loop of yarn through to right side.

3 Holding contrast yarn on wrong side, insert hook into crochet 1 stitch below and pull another loop of yarn to right side, taking it through both crochet and loop already on hook to make slip stitch.

4 Continue in this way, working around slipper and making 1 slip stitch in each hole between slipper stitches until round is complete. Secure yarn on wrong side in same way as Step 1. Repeat with 3 remaining colors, spacing rounds 1 stitch apart.

chapter 6
gallery

The Gallery contains a photograph of **every accessory and variation** in the book. The projects are grouped so that accessories of the same type are shown together, making it easy to see the kinds of embellishments used. **Browse** through the pictures and enjoy working out what you'll choose to make for your next crochet project, but don't forget that there are many **more combinations** you can create using the techniques in the book. Try adding fluffy pompoms to a felted bag, stitch chunky beads or brightly colored buttons onto a hat, or work bands of glittering sequins on a scarf—the **choice** is yours.

SCARVES

Copper, page 56

Scarf with ball buttons and loops

Erica, page 58

Scarf with strip closure

Susie, page 32

Narrow scarf with pom-poms

Priscilla, page 34

Scarf with shell edging

Jazz, page 36

Scarf with granny square

pockets

Elegant, page 78

Scarf with crocheted-in beads

Patience, page 106

Lacy shell scarf

SCARF VARIATIONS

Looped scarf, page 51

Scarf with looped edging

Pyramid, page 80

Scarf with beaded felt circles

Fringed scarf, page 41

Scarf with yarn fringe

Button scarf, page 87

Scarf with button trim

Paris, page 82

Scarf with beaded fringe

Ruffled scarf, page 45

Scarf with ruffle

Curly scarf, page 95

Scarf with curlicue fringe

BAGS

Summer, page 38

Bag with crochet flower trim

Arizona, page 40

Bag with yarn fringe

Orient, page 60

Bag with bamboo handles

Hearts, page 62

Bag with grab handles

Lauren, page 64 (right)

Clutch bag with triangular flap

Snowflake, page 84

Felted bag with sequins

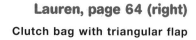

Nordic, page 86

Felted bag decorated with buttons

Glitter, page 100

Small evening bag

Sarah, page 104

Mesh tote bag

Pocket bag, page 37

Bag with granny square pocket

Button and loop bag, page 56

Bag with ball buttons and loops

Amanda, page 110

Plastic shoulder bag

Glamorous bag, page 43

Bag with marabou trim

Shallow bag, page 61

Bag with painted wooden handles

Violet, page 114

Felted bag

Felt-trimmed bag, page 53

Bag with pinked felt strips

Shoulder bag, page 63

Bag with shoulder strap

Toggle bag, page 67

Bag with toggle fastening

Tab bag, page 75

Bag with hook-and-loop

fastening

Felted bag with handles, page 109

Punk bag, page 69

Bag with decorative zippers

Glitzy bag, page 83

Bag with beaded fringe

Felted bag with shoulder strap, page 109

Braided bag, page 71

Bag with braided fastening

Hearts and stars, page 89

Bag decorated with jewels

Felted bag with loop fastening, page 109

HATS

College, page 46

Hat with crab stitch edging

Anna, page 70

Hat with crochet braids

Flapper, page 72 (below)

Hat with earflaps

Molly, page 92

Hat with ring buttons

Curly, page 94

Hat with curlicues

Topknot, page 48

Hat with crochet tassel

Loopy, page 50

Hat with looped edging

Happy, page 102

Stocking hat with pom-poms

Cozy, page 108

Hat with stripes

HAT VARIATIONS

Appliqué hat, page 81

Hat with beaded felt circles

MITTENS

Fluffy, page 42

Shortie mittens with marabou
trim

Florence, page 44

Mittens with ruffled cuff

Toggle, page 66

Mittens with toggle fastening

Snappy, page 68

Shortie mittens with decorative
zipper

Jewel, page 88

Mittens with jewel trim

Liberty, page 90

mittens with shells and bells

Amy, page 112

Mittens with contrast cuffs

SLIPPERS

Zigzag, page 52

Slippers with felt trim

Spice, page 116

Slippers with surface crochet

MITTEN VARIATIONS

Glitzy mittens, page 85

Mittens with sequin decoration

Sporty, page 74

Slippers with tab fastening

SLIPPER VARIATIONS

Shell-edged slippers, page 35

Slippers with shell edging

Ring mittens, page 93

Mittens with ring buttons

Charming, page 96

Slippers with novelty charms

Edged slippers, page 47

Slippers with crab stitch edging

Index

Acknowledgments

Breslich & Foss Ltd and Jan Eaton would like to thank the following individuals for their help in the creation of this book: Alicia Ryan and Tashi Archdale for modeling the accessories; Jackie Jones for styling the hair and makeup; Martin Norris for all the photography; Hazel Williams for checking the patterns and Marie Clayton for editorial assistance. Last but not least, our thanks go to designer Elizabeth Healey, whose original concept this series was.